THE TRANSFORMATIONAL FRAMEWORK

the
Transformational Framework

A process tool for the development of Transformational games

Written & Developed By

Sabrina Culyba

SCHELLGAMES

Acknowledgements

The Transformational Framework and this book have both evolved over a number of years from the experiences and input of many individuals and teams.

First, thanks to **Lynn Fiellin, MD**, and her team at the Yale University School of Medicine and the play2PREVENT Lab, particularly **Kimberly Hieftje, PhD** and **Lindsay Duncan, PhD**. The early roots of inspiration for this Framework can be traced to the Game PlayBooks that Yale and Schell Games collaboratively developed in 2011 for the PlayForward project. Thanks also to **Ben Sawyer**, of Digitalmill, for his work with Yale and Schell Games in shepherding the PlayForward project.

Also inspirational in the early creation of this Framework was the work of **Barbara Chamberlin** (Project Director of the NMSU Learning Games Lab), **Jesús Trespalacios** (NMSU), and **Rachel Gallagher** (NMSU) in their 2012 paper in the International Journal of Game-Based Learning, *The Learning Games Design Model: Immersion, Collaboration, and Outcomes-Driven Development*.

Many teams have used some version of this book and the Transformational Framework since 2012. Often these teams were working with book drafts that were woefully incomplete. Thank you especially to the studio members of **Schell Games** for using iterations of the Framework and generously giving of their time to share their struggles and ideas for working on Transformational games. In particular, I'd like to thank the team members and partners of these projects: **Ivy, Lexica, STEM, Nightshift, Happy Atoms, Odyssey, Anti-bully, Scrubs, Mechanisms, Parks**, and **Fancy Hat**. Thank you also to **Anisha Deshmane** and **Charles Amis** for their time reviewing drafts and sharing comments.

Additional thanks to the students and faculty at **Carnegie Mellon's Entertainment Technology Center** who, since 2014, have been using the Framework and this book on many of their Transformational student projects. Their positive experiences helped me believe this book would be helpful for others.

A book like this is not possible to complete without support. I'd like to extend special thanks to the following cheerleaders and contributors:

Harley Baldwin – who saw the value in the Framework's development and encouraged its growth at Schell Games, who supported the writing of this book, and who contributed her own insights into the audiences beyond the player. **Barbara Chamberlin** – who read an early rough draft and became an encouraging cheerleader, and whose own work was an early inspiration for the Framework. **drew davidson** – who was everlastingly patient while i worked on this book and never missed a chance to ask me how it was going. **Kate Gigliotti-Gordon** – who helped me navigate the rules of grammar and punctuation. **Yotam Haimberg** – for putting the original Framework through its paces on *Happy Atoms*, resulting in several additions and iterations, as well as his feedback on subsequent drafts of this book and for contributing a developer story. **Jessica Hammer** – whose enthusiasm to use the book with her students helped motivate the book's completion, who reviewed several drafts and provided insightful comments, and who contributed a developer story from her own design work. **Brad King (and ETC Press)** – for providing a publishing platform that supports works like this. **Michal Ksiazkiewicz** – who has led several projects using the Framework, providing feedback along the way, and who contributed a developer story. **Brooke Morrill** – who has shepherded many Transformational games into existence at Schell Games, and who contributed especially to the grant and research information, including a developer story. **Shawn Patton** – for his successful final hour typo hunting. **Jason Pratt** – for his contribution of a developer story and his invaluable proofreading. **Anna Roberts** – for her insight into human-centered and collaborative design, for her hours and hours of feedback and review of book chapters, and for always reminding me about the power of getting comfortable with being uncomfortable. **Jesse Schell** – for being a generous mentor, the first advocate of the term "transformational," and for creating the kind of studio where this work could be explored. **Emily Treat** – for her contribution of a developer story.

Most of all, my heartfelt gratitude to **David Culyba**,
my partner in all things.
From your work using the Framework with your students
to our many, many long conversations,
your influence is written into every page of this book.
Your insight and patience are an endless well of support.

Why this book?

I wrote this book to contribute something to the development process of Transformational games. It outlines the Transformational Framework, a pre-production tool that originally arose at Schell Games to empower teams working on these kinds of games. The book explains the pieces of this process and provides supporting strategies and insights.

The primary intended audience of this book is experienced video game developers moving from entertainment-focused games to Transformational games, particularly individuals in leadership and design roles. It's also intended reading for clients and partners working on Transformational games.

Students and those new to game development will also benefit from reading; however, this book does not focus on how to design good gameplay. (In my opinion, you won't find a better introduction to that topic than Jesse Schell's *Art of Game Design*.)

In this book, I am implicitly referring to video games whenever I use the term "game," though other forms of games, or game-like experiences, with transformational aspirations may find the Framework to be relevant as well.

The Transformational Framework is a model. It is not a set of absolute rules or perfect answers to the challenges of creating Transformational games. As the saying goes, "*All models are wrong, but some are useful.*" (Thank you, George Box.)

If I could reach back in time and give myself a tool for my own early Transformational game projects, it would be this book. I hope it proves useful for you.

- Sabrina Culyba

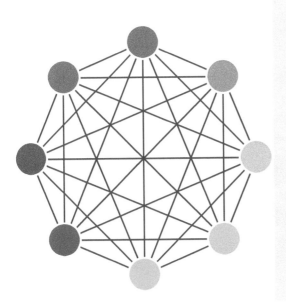

Defining the Problem

Trans·for·ma·tion·al
/ ˌtran(t)sfər ' māSH(ə)n(ə)l/

Many games – including mainstream games intended primarily as entertainment – can trigger transformational experiences that change players. If any game has the potential to be transformational, what specific games are we referring to when we use the term "Transformational games?"

For references on the transformative power of games, see Appendix A.

The challenge facing game developers in this space is not whether or not game experiences have the potential to transform players. The challenge is designing a game, from the ground up, to achieve a particular intended transformation. In this book, we use "Transformational" with a capital "T" to refer to games created with this specific intention.

Let's start by examining further what characterizes a Transformational game. Then we'll look at some of the challenges faced by teams working on these games and why the Transformational Framework was created.

Entertainment vs Transformational

We use the term "Transformational" to refer to games designed with the **intention** to change players in some way. In further defining Transformational games, it can help to start from the familiar space of entertainment games.

In typical entertainment games, we focus on the player inside the game world. We use our game design tools to direct the player's attention and behavior inside the game. The game is its own reality, and what matters is how the player engages with that reality. Our purpose is typically to design a game that is appealing enough to draw players in, clear enough to understand how to play, and deep enough to encourage sustained engagement in the game. Playing an entertainment game may cause a change in players beyond the game, but that change is incidental and not our focus as designers. Of course, players *do* change while inside an entertainment game – they learn skills and change their behavior to meet the game's challenges – but these changes revolve around their interaction with the game itself.

In Transformational games, we focus on the player *beyond* the game. For Transformational games, if the player changes inside the game – for example, changes behavior or gains a skill – but this change only manifests inside the game, then we have not succeeded. Our goal is for the player to demonstrate this change outside the game context. We call this application of player change from the game world to the real world **transfer**.

Likewise, if the player exhibits a change while still engaging with the game but these changes disappear once the game experience ends, then we have not succeeded. Our goal is to create change that is not dependent on the player continuing to play the game. We call this aspect **persistence**.

INTENTION

The game is purposefully designed to create a specific change.

TRANSFER

The change extends into the real world.

PERSISTENCE

The change remains after the game is over.

Transformational Games are those games developed with the **intention** of changing players in a specific way that **transfers** and **persists** beyond the game.

Some Examples of Transformational Games

At Risk
Developer: Kognito
This role-play simulation aims to increase awareness, reduce stigma, and facilitate conversations related to mental illness.

Bury Me, My Love
Developer: The Pixel Hunt/Figs/ARTE France
This instant messaging adventure game aims to give players empathy and insight into the experience of Syrian refugees.

DragonBox Algebra 12+
Developer: DragonBox
This puzzle game is designed to teach children the concepts of basic algebra.

Duolingo
Developer: Duolingo
This game-styled language learning platform was created with the goal of allowing anyone to learn a new language.

Happy Atoms
Developer: Schell Games
This tablet game, paired with a physical toy, is designed to demystify chemistry by giving players a hands-on way to explore the structure of molecules and their applications.

Harness Heroes
Developer: Simcoach Games
This mobile game about fall protection was designed as part of the larger Simcoach Skill Arcade suite to inspire and connect youth to relevant career paths in American industries where skill gaps are common.

Never Alone (Kisima Inṇitchuṇa)
Developer: Upper One Games, E-Line Media
This puzzle platformer aims to showcase and cultivate interest in the culture and folklore of the Iñupiat Native Alaskan people.

This list is only a tiny sampling of Transformational games.
The games listed here cover many different topics, gameplay genres, and
audiences. They come from a variety of developers, each with their own
unique development process, but each was developed with the intention
of transforming players.

Phone Story
Developer: Molleindustria
This collection of four minigames aims to
provoke the player's reflection on the
hidden negative human cost in mobile
phone manufacturing.

PlayForward®: Elm City Stories
Developer: play2PREVENT®, Schell Games
This tablet game aims to reduce HIV
exposure in at-risk teens by changing
their skills, knowledge, and behaviors
around risky situations.

Re-Mission
Developer: Hopelab, Realtime Associates
This series of games was designed
specifically for kids with cancer to
boost their self-efficacy and improve
their treatment adherence.

SuperBetter
Developer: SuperBetter
This game-like tool was created to help
players build up their personal resilience
to overcome challenges and reach
personal goals.

The End
Developer: Preloaded
This web-game for teens was designed
to make death easier to deal with by
prompting reflection on questions about
life and mortality.

Win the White House
Developer: Filament Games, iCivics
This game is designed to introduce
players to the process and strategy
behind the American presidential election.

For links to each
of these games,
see Appendix B.

Zombies, Run!
Developer: Six to Start & Naomi Alderman
This audio adventure game was created
to motivate players to run and exercise.

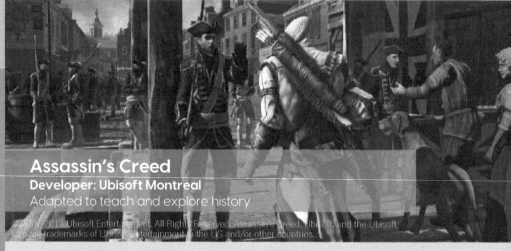

Assassin's Creed
Developer: Ubisoft Montreal
Adapted to teach and explore history

Gone Home
Developer: Fullbright
Adapted to teach English language arts skills

Minecraft
Developer: Mojang
Adapted for many subjects

A few examples of commercial games adapted for transformational purposes beyond their original intent.

Intentionally Designed vs. Adapted

What about an entertainment game that a teacher adapts for their classroom setting? Or a game through which players can develop incidental real-world skills, such as using math to figure out optimal character builds in a role-playing game? It's certainly valuable to learn from these examples.

Adaptation takes what is already created and tries to re-harness it for a different purpose than what was originally intended. This can be a powerful strategy for anyone seeking to transform players through games. One benefit is the ability to choose from the most popular games, so that we can have confidence in the game's engagement. There's probably no stronger recent example of this potential than the game of *Minecraft*, which has been adapted for all sorts of transformational purposes.

For resources on adapting games, see Appendix C.

Adaptation does have its limitations, however. We often can't change the content or function of a digital game. Instead, any inaccuracies, omissions, or distracting, unrelated mechanics have to be addressed by structure outside the game, such as curricular materials. Further, there are many topics that conventional entertainment games rarely touch upon.

We should not just rely on sifting through entertainment games, looking for something with enough structure and flexibility to be adapted for a transformational purpose.

By combining the game design process with a transformational design process, we can address limitations that result from adaptation and support the goals of transformation inherently in the experience we create.

It's noteworthy that two of the examples to the left (both Assassin's Creed and Minecraft) have released game editions specifically developed for education *after* communities formed around the use of those games for transformational purposes.

For more info related to these examples, see Appendix D.

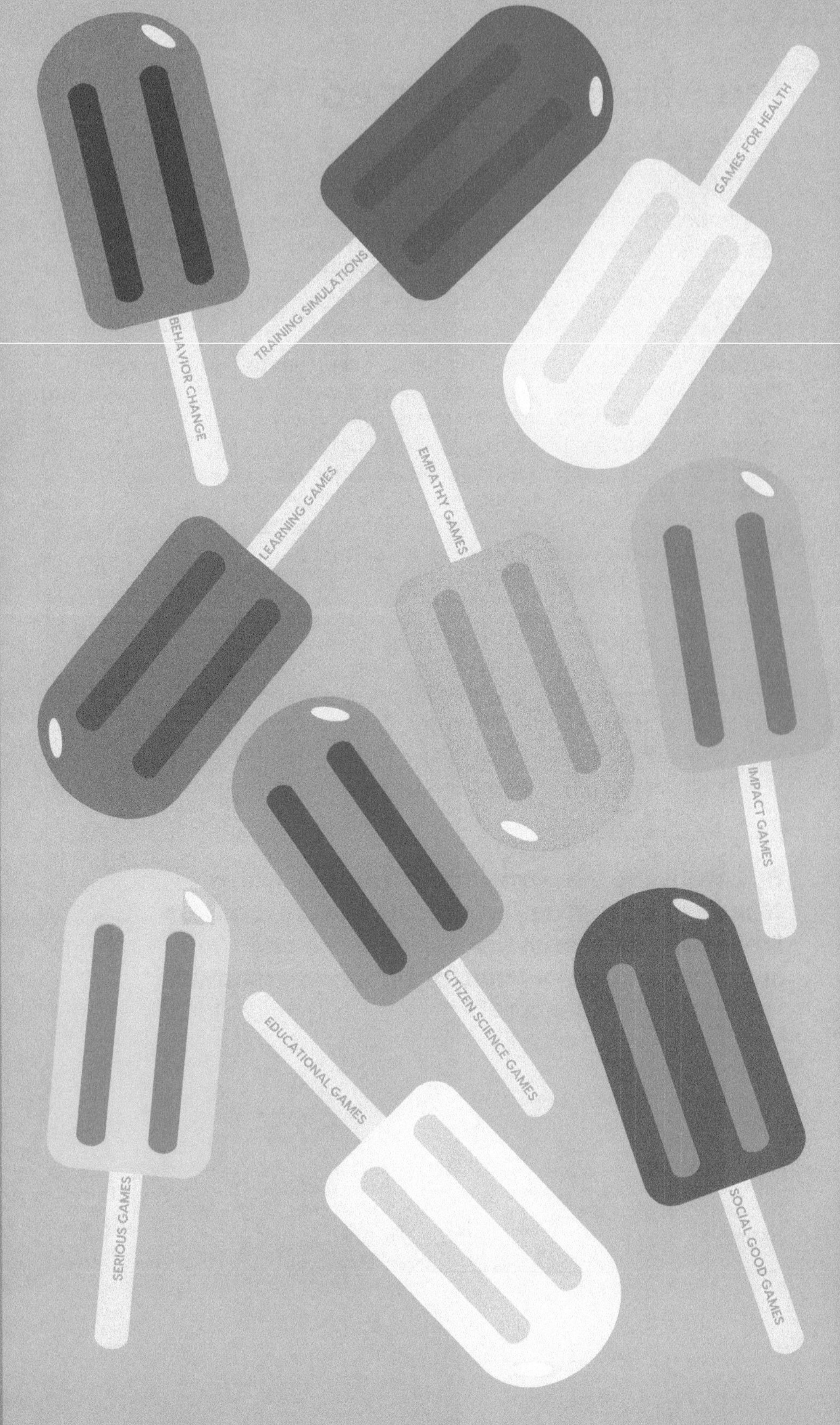
BEHAVIOR CHANGE
TRAINING SIMULATIONS
GAMES FOR HEALTH
LEARNING GAMES
EMPATHY GAMES
IMPACT GAMES
CITIZEN SCIENCE GAMES
EDUCATIONAL GAMES
SERIOUS GAMES
SOCIAL GOOD GAMES

Flavors of Transformational

"Transformational" is meant to be an inclusive term that can apply to any game where the intention is to change the player.

Here are a number of other game terms that also typically classify as Transformational games:

- **Educational Games/Learning Games**
  These labels are usually applied to games targeting students, often children, both in and out of a classroom setting.

- **Serious Games**
  This generally catch-all term is used in many different contexts for any game that has a real-world purpose beyond entertainment.

- **Training Simulations/Simulation-based Learning**
  Frequently used in reference to programs that train employees on technical skills, industry procedures, or social interactions through simulation and role-play.

- **Behavior Change Games**
  This term seems to be used most often in games initiated in part as research, particularly around health-related behaviors.

- **Games for Health**
  As the name suggests, this term refers to games aimed at improving health-related behaviors and outcomes

- **Impact Games/Social Good Games/Games for Change**
  These games are often trying to raise awareness about a societal issue or cause.

- **Empathy Games**
  This term is sometimes applied to games that focus less on game mechanics and more on storytelling. They are often centered around evoking an emotional response in players.

- **Citizen Science/Crowdsourcing Games**
  These are games that allow the masses to contribute to real-world research or data analysis by encoding the tasks into a game.

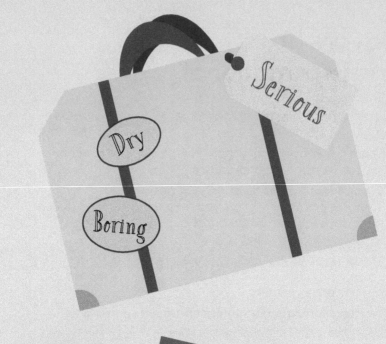

Serious

Dry

Boring

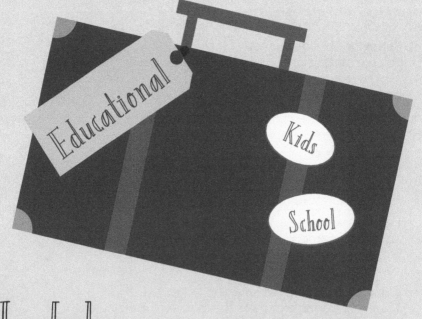

Educational

Kids

School

Labels
Have
Baggage

Labels Can Transform Thinking

To some, it might seem silly or even counter-productive to promote "Transformational" as the term of choice when there are already more generally accepted terms – notably "Educational" or "Serious." However, the labels we use can influence our thinking and the thinking of others.

"Serious Games" implies an emphasis on the tone of the game experience. Although it may make investing in such games more palatable to anyone still nervous about supporting the use of "games" in training, healthcare, or schools, it holds us hostage to the misguided idea that learning and self-betterment must be tedious or boring work. Playfulness, surprise, delight, fantasy, humor, etc. can all play a powerful role in transformative experiences. We don't have to be serious for games to provide meaning beyond fun.

The phrase "Educational Games" narrows our view of the kinds of topics we can tackle and the audiences we can reach through these games. The word "educational" bends thoughts toward skills and knowledge normally connected with formal education – math, science, reading, language. Through these existing strong associations, the label "educational" discourages connections to the broader human experience – topics like socioemotional skills, religious beliefs, social justice, perspective taking, mental & physical health, cultural heritage, etc. It also tends to focus our attention on younger audiences who exist inside a traditional classroom setting.

"Transformational" calls out a game's emphasis on creating player change rather than its topic, tone, or audience. Player change can take many forms and target many different audiences. As you read this book, try embracing the use of the term "Transformational" and see if it opens up possibilities in your thinking about what we could do with our medium.

Overheard on Transformational Games

I don't know anything about this stuff!

How will we really know if this works?

Our priorities seem to keep shifting..

What should we be doing differently from entertainment game dev?

Shouldn't we be talking to an expert?

There are so many stakeholders!

How do we get our game to the people that really need it?

What's really critical to include in the game?

Our client doesn't understand games!

What if people love our game but it doesn't work?

What if our game works but no one wants to play it?

What's more important: the fun or the learning?

Isn't there some research out there we should be looking at?

What actually matters for success?

What claims can we really make about our game's impact?

I don't feel like I can contribute to changing players....

I don't understand some of our design decisions...

How do we get teachers to adopt our game?

Wow, this is a lot of content to integrate in our game...

How should we work with our subject-matter expert?

The Challenges
You Will Face

If you've previously worked on a Transformational game, you probably recognize many of the statements to the left. If you will be working on a Transformational game for the first time, take a moment to read over these sentiments. These are some of the frustrations and insecurities that are experienced by teams working on these games.

Teams embarking on Transformational games for the first time may be blind to the new challenges they will face. Your team will encounter unfamiliar challenges when working on Transformational games. You may be working with content you don't fully understand. You will struggle with balancing the desire to iterate towards the most fun player experience and the need to create a game that effectively changes players. You will likely find unusual and surprising constraints that your design must accommodate but that may not be obvious at the start of development. These issues and more create tension about priorities and success when working on these games.

The first step to empowering you and your team during development is to expect the extra challenges you will face. This foreknowledge will not necessarily eliminate these challenges, but you and your team can face them with the confidence that when these problems arise, it is not because you are doing something wrong, but, in fact, because you are struggling with what many teams face when working on these kinds of games.

Create Space to Define the Problem

Knowing to expect these challenges helps teams cope when they appear, but what we really want to do is get ahead of these problems so that we can mitigate or avoid them.

Many frustrations on Transformational games stem from failing to establish a shared vision of the design problem with stakeholders and team members. In entertainment game development, there is an industry mindset that the sooner you have something playable, the sooner you can start iterating on what's fun. In Transformational games, before you dive into game development, you should set aside some time for you and your team to gain a deep, shared understanding of your design problem. Your problem is not just making a fun game. It is also making a game that transforms players in a specific way. Not just any fun game will do and also not just any transformation will do.

Creating and protecting space to deeply understand your design problem is not always easy, and, for many teams, it is new. It can be especially hard for teams coming from traditional entertainment games. You're experienced developers, so you know how to make a good game, right? But how experienced are you at teaching teens to make better life choices? Or designing for teachers to integrate your game into their classrooms? You and your team have to first accept that your existing game development process and experience might not be enough.

Games (and this goes especially for Transformational games) are often created under constrained deadlines and budgets. Under these conditions, it can be difficult to commit time for this sort of work when resources are already limited.

This work will require time and effort, but the benefit is a team that is more prepared for their journey together.

Stop for Wisdom

Think of the development of your game as setting out to climb a tall mountain. The Transformational Framework process is a sort of basecamp – stop here with your team to learn more about the terrain ahead and make sure you have the supplies you need. Your journey will still have unknowns and risks, but the preparation you do here will help your team to know what to expect and make it safely to the top.

IT'S DANGEROUS
TO GO ALONE!

TAKE THIS.

Throughout this book,
you'll see this medallion
used to represent the
Transformational
Framework.

Use This Framework to Jumpstart

So how do you set about creating a shared vision of your transformational design problem? If you believe you need to set aside time for this effort, how should you spend this time? What questions do you need to answer? What conversations do you need to have? What research do you need to do?

There's no perfect, complete, or right answer to these questions, but the Transformational Framework is a model you can use as a springboard for your own process.

The Framework is, at its core, a set of exploratory questions covering eight critical topics for Transformational games. It includes an evolving shared vocabulary and taxonomy for these topics so that you, your team, and your stakeholders can work together with a common language. This Framework guide also includes some tips, warnings, and best practices for working on Transformational games.

The Framework was created with insight from some of those who have gone before you and wrestled with some of the same challenges you are likely to face. The Framework grew out of work at Schell Games, a studio that has worked on a variety of Transformational games for over a decade. Many teams at Schell Games have used the Transformational Framework in some form or another since 2013. It has also been used by student teams at Carnegie Mellon's Entertainment Technology Center. The Framework is intended to be a distillation of lessons learned from these prior efforts and experiences.

The Framework is open for adoption, adaptation, and evolution. This book is intended to serve as a standalone introduction to the Transformational Framework for all people involved in the game development process: team leaders and other team members, as well as clients, experts, and other partners. It is offered, not as a rigid ruleset, but as an evolving template for teams to integrate into their unique process and circumstances.

Where to Go Next:

Game Development Primer

If you're new to game development, check out the game development primer in the next section before continuing to the Transformational Framework.

Framework Overview

To start learning about the Transformational Framework, jump ahead to the Framework Overview Chapter

Side Quest

Game
Development
Primer

The video game industry is a relatively young and diverse industry. There's no one model that perfectly captures how games are developed. There are, however, some common practices, concepts, and realities with which most who've worked in games are familiar.

If you're new to game development (or "game dev" as you might hear it called), this primer will not make you an expert, but it will expose you to some important game development concepts.

If you are a client, teacher, subject-matter expert, or other non-game dev partner working with a game development team ("dev team"), this primer aims to arm you with the lingo and high-level knowledge you need to keep up in conversations with the dev team.

Experienced devs might find it useful to skim this section to understand what kinds of concepts would be helpful for your partners to understand about game development.

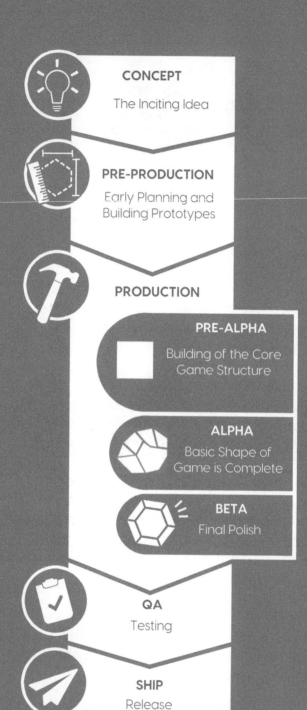

The Game Development Process

The game development process can be messy and diverse in practice, but at the high level it typically has five phases:

1. Concept
The idea of the game is first being imagined. Sometimes this stage includes a pitch process where the game idea is presented to key decision-makers and funders. At this point, the team might be quite small and may not include the people who will actually work on the game production.

Transformational games often start with a real-world need to be addressed, rather than a game concept.

2. Pre-production
The initial proving ground for the game concept and production plan. Often this period involves a lot of exploration and iteration, including creating playable prototypes of key technology, mechanics, or content. At this point, the team is likely to be a subset of the eventual full team. Some pre-productions end with a "greenlight" pitch, where a project is either given the go-ahead or shelved.

This is where creating the Transformational Framework is the most useful.

3. Production
The full team is brought on board to build the game. Often production is broken into stages:

- **Pre-Alpha:** This is the period when the core pieces of the game start to take shape. During this time, prototyping is still very common and big shifts can occur as early ideas about the game direction are tested and explored.

- **Alpha:** The core game works but not all features are complete. Content is usually incomplete, and it is likely that some significant changes and iteration will be desirable.

- **Beta:** The game is largely functionally complete and content is representative of the quantity and quality that will be in the final game. At this point, the focus is on polishing what is in the game, rather than adding new elements or making significant changes.

4. QA (Quality Assurance)
This stage is dedicated to testing the game rigorously and fixing any problems (bugs) that are found.

5. Ship (Publish)
The game is released. This often is not the end of work as ongoing support, game updates, and community interaction may continue after this point.

Paper Prototype
A cardboard mockup of a level in the virtual reality game
I Expect You To Die by Schell Games

White Box
A screenshot for a white box prototype of a level in
I Expect You To Die by Schell Games

Iteration, Playtests, & Prototypes

If there is one value critical to game design and development, it is iteration. Iteration is the practice of building something, testing it, evaluating its results, making changes, and testing again. Game developers know that the first version of any game or game system is often confusing, broken, and generally not fun. It is only through iteration that great games can be developed.

For an illustrative account of real game iteration, see Appendix E.

Playtesting is the engine of iteration in game development. Playtesting is putting prototypes or the game itself in front of players, observing their reaction, and using these observations to make development decisions. Good game development uses playtests early and often.

For more on playtesting, see Appendix F.

Prototyping is the art of building just enough to test an idea. A prototype is a mockup or simplified version of an idea. Game development uses prototypes to iterate more quickly by building something quick and dirty to test. Here are a few terms that refer to specialized types of prototypes:

- **Paper Prototype:** This is a non-digital prototype. It is by far the cheapest way to prototype. (Note that it doesn't have to actually use paper!)
  E.g., A team is creating an avatar customization system for their game and wondering which items would most excite players. They could create a paper prototype of their concepts and have a playtest where players create a paper doll version of an avatar to see what items are most popular with players.

- **White Box:** A term used for a mock-up of part of a game using simplified objects.
  E.g., A team is working on a first-person shooter. They create a white box of each level with unfinished models to playtest ideas before deciding on final level layouts.

- **Sandbox:** A tool that allows developers to quickly change and test settings in order to prototype portions of the game.
  E.g., A team is working on a role-playing game where lots of different battles need to be designed. They build a sandbox tool that allows their designers to quickly prototype different combinations of enemies.

- **Vertical Slice:** A playable version of a complete section of the game that demonstrates the target final look and feel. This kind of "prototype" is most like production and so requires more resources. It's typically used to confirm (or "greenlight") the full production plan of a game.

Game Development Teams

Video game development is an interdisciplinary endeavor. It has a wide range of team sizes, from solo "indie" developers to teams with hundreds of people. Here are some of the roles commonly found on game dev teams:

- **Artists:** These team members can encompass a very diverse set of talents, from concept art to 3D modeling to animation to lighting and special effects.

- **Audio Designers:** These team members are responsible for the audio experience of the game, including sound effects, voice over, and music.

- **Engineers:** These team members write the code that brings the game to life. Engineers tackle the challenging programming and hardware problems that must be solved to enable a great game experience.

- **Game Designers:** These team members are responsible for the player's experience. With input from team and playtesting, designers make decisions about the game features and ensure that the team has clear understanding of what they are building. Designers often fill specialized content roles such as Level Designer or Writer.

- **Producers:** These team members could be thought of as the team's shepherds. A producer ensures the team stays on target to deliver a finished, quality product within the time and resources available. They handle team needs, wrangle the schedule, and often serve as liaison to clients and publishers.

- **UX Designers:** This role (User Experience) is responsible for the design of the interfaces in the game. They focus on how the player interacts with the game as well as how they receive feedback.

- **Quality Assurance:** These team members provide testing for the game. They work with the team to create test plans and then run the game through these tests, documenting any issues they discover so that the team can address them.

- **Marketing:** Often a huge portion of game budgets on blockbuster games, marketing is responsible for getting the word out about the game and driving sales. This may include creating additional assets like trailers, press releases, etc. It can also include attending trade shows, participating in festivals, posting on social media, and making commercial announcements.

- **Community Manager:** Some game teams have members dedicated to cultivating the game's player community. This could mean responding to comments through sales channels, moderating game forums, running special in-game events, or reaching out to players through social media.

- **Publisher:** Indie developers and independent studios may self-publish, meaning they fund and market the games they make themselves. Other games are made in partnership with a publisher, who often largely funds the game and may take on a large part of the marketing. Depending on the arrangement with the developer, publishers can have more or less of an active influence over the design of the game.

On small teams, some of these roles may be handled by the same person while on big teams, some may be split into even more specialized divisions.

Design

Art

Audio

Production

Engineering

QA

UX Design

Marketing

Community
Management

Publishing

*Though these are common roles on developer teams,
the exact titles, specializations, and hierarchies of each
varies across the game development industry.*

Innovative
Features

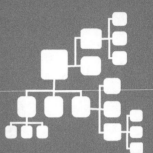

Lots of
Systems

LEVELS,
ANIMATION,
NARRATIVE,
VOICE OVER,
ETC.

Content
Heavy

Multiple
Platforms

Multiplayer

Scoping
Your Game

Game production is about managing risk. Video games are complex systems, often pursuing new, unique experiences or pushing the limits of the latest technology. Central to understanding risk in game production is this question: *How many unknowns remain for you to solve?* An unknown can range from a technical problem to details of the game design. Unknowns represent risk along all three main components of video game production: **Scope**, **Schedule**, and **Budget**.

Scope describes the work required to develop the game. Predicting the scope of a full game or one of its features isn't an exact science, but here are some generalities:

- **New, innovative features that are very unique to your game can have unclear costs.** The cost of a feature is a factor of both what it takes to build the feature initially plus the iteration it takes to get it feeling great. New, unique features increase the risk that your team will need to iterate quite a bit to figure out the details of how those features should work for players. Sometimes a small feature that requires a lot of iteration can end up being more work than a big feature with a very clear implementation.

- **The more systems you have in your game, the bigger the scope.** More systems means more stuff to build. More systems also means more interactions between systems, with more opportunities for complex edge cases and bugs. It also means more functionality to explain to the player which impacts both tutorials (on-boarding) and playtesting.

- **Content can balloon scope significantly**, especially if you plan to rely on extensive writing, animation, or voice acting.

Some problems in game development are known to significantly increase scope. There are some problems that are nearly always particularly thorny to tackle in game development. Here are two examples:

- **Launch on multiple hardware platforms:** Although a lot of progress has been made on tools that help teams build the same game for multiple platforms (e.g., Android, iPhone, PC, web, etc.), it is still true that each additional platform you support will come with unique problems to solve.

- **Include multiplayer:** Allowing players to interact with one another can extend the game experience, but it also requires significant technical systems and can add a lot of complexity to the game's design and testing.

Game Schedules

- Frontload Unknowns
- Built Around Milestones
- Often Change Through Development

Game Budgets

- Bigger Than Expected
- The Marketing Budget Matters

Schedules & Budgets

Game schedules are often designed to front-load creative and technical risks. The iterative development process is, in part, a way the industry has developed to mitigate risk by encouraging teams to build quickly towards a playable game and then continue playtesting throughout development to ensure they are heading in a good direction. One strategy is to build the parts of the game with the most unknowns first, so that there is time to iterate on these parts.

Most game schedules use some form of milestones that act as checkpoints on how the game development is progressing. This typically involves an in-progress build of the game showing a targeted set of features and content. Although teams may outline a full schedule of milestones at the start of the project, keep in mind that, due to the iterative nature of game development, it's not uncommon for the details of milestone deliveries to change as the game evolves.

Game budgets are bigger than you think. Many people new to game development are surprised at the cost. Remember, reflecting on scope and risk as discussed so far, the budget has to cover the final game **and** every iteration of the game that you'll throw away before you figure out that final version. Want a cheaper game?

- **Go 2D.** 3D content is typically (though not always) more expensive to author and iterate with than 2D games because of the added complexity of world design, animation, navigation, technical performance, etc.

- **Remix mechanics from existing games.** Scope is more predictable and usually smaller if you already know exactly how the game should work. By mimicking parts of an existing game, in whole or in part, you can reduce the risk of scope ballooning from iteration, and thus reduce cost. Most games incorporate mechanics and pieces of design from prior games, but very closely copying a full game is called "cloning" and is generally frowned upon.

Want a blockbuster game? Your marketing budget matters. One unexpectedly large part of blockbuster game budgets is marketing, which can be as big as (if not bigger than) the development budget.

Psst!

What Developers Want You To Know

"Everyone" is not a target audience. Your dev team will likely ask you to define a target audience. It's common for clients to answer "we'd like it to be for everyone." This is **not** a realistic target audience. A target audience helps your team make better design decisions by establishing their most important players. This audience is usually distinguished by attributes like age, gender, motivation, lifestyle, and gameplay preferences. Setting a target audience does not mean that other players are necessarily excluded.

It's not always obvious what things are hard (expensive) versus easy (cheap.) Ask! It can be surprising which features can be easily added and which would be quite difficult. It can depend on the expertise of your particular team or the details of the existing game systems. If you are a client or partner, don't assume something is easy or hard. Talk to your dev team and ask questions. Focus on expressing the motivation for your request. What problem are you trying to solve? Often focusing on the problem, instead of a specific solution, can allow a development team to come up with a creative (and in-scope) way to address the concern.

Unknown requirements or constraints create development risk and friction. Teams don't like to be surprised by unexpected requirements or feel like they are working under unknown rules. Take time to gather and honestly communicate constraints or requirements as soon as you are aware of them. Some examples:

- **An upcoming demo requirement:** There are resource costs to preparing an in-progress game build to show well at a demo. Don't surprise your dev team with a last-minute request. Give them enough notice to prepare.

- **Key stakeholder requirement or trigger:** For example, if you know that an important stakeholder really dislikes a particular animal and the use of that animal might impact their approval of the game, let your dev team know. (It sounds silly, but this kind of thing really does happen.)

Remember, it is okay and even expected for the occasional schedule change or new requirement to pop up. Keep these to a minimum and communicate them as soon as possible so your dev team has time to make adjustments and alert you to potential implications to scope, schedule, or budget.

Part of managing risk is making cuts. You will almost definitely need to cut scope at some point in development, and that means making a call to remove a game system or trim your content. The further you are in your development schedule, the riskier it is to be working on features where you are uncertain what it will take to make them good enough. Consider cutting these features in favor of applying more resources to make the other parts of the game stronger and more polished. It's almost always better to cut proactively and intentionally than to find yourself just running out of time or going over budget at the end.

Have a clear, short chain of approval. Make sure everyone on it makes time to see the game at critical milestones. Every project benefits when it is clear who sets approvals and whose feedback has highest priority. Developers want clarity on when something is approved or not. They want to know who has final say on a feature. Take time to map out this approval hierarchy at the start of the project and make sure that your schedule includes in-progress milestones where everyone, including the highest-level decision maker, will review the game and provide feedback. Set a single person who is responsible for ensuring these reviews happen and who is gathering this feedback and facilitating these approvals.

Late feedback is the worst feedback. Experienced developers will expect to get both positive and negative feedback. Be professionally polite, but also honest about what you like and don't like about the game. Expect to occasionally get pushback on feedback, either because your development team has a particular recommendation as developers, or because limited resources simply don't allow every piece of feedback to be addressed.

You'll need to pick your battles. If you're a client or partner with many internal voices, it's often a good idea to get some internal consensus on feedback before passing it along to the development team. But the absolute most important rule to follow with feedback is to provide it in a timely manner. The worst situation for everyone is when feedback is given and it's too late to make changes without serious repercussions.

The
Transformational
Framework

Overview of the Transformational Framework

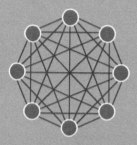

What's in the
Framework and how
should it be used?

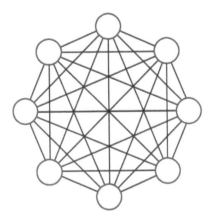

The Transformational Framework is a process grounded in an intersecting set of exploratory questions intended to help teams build a shared vision of their design problem. Its purpose is to help you and your team ask (and answer!) both broad and deep questions about your transformational goals and how those goals might be accomplished through your game.

The Framework is intended as a pre-production tool, used before you make design decisions about your game experience. It will continue to inform your game development throughout production.

There are eight pieces to the Transformational Framework. This first chapter gives a high-level overview of the entire Framework and how to approach it. Then each piece of the Framework is covered in detail in the following chapters.

What's in the Framework?

Each piece of the Framework connects back to the common challenges experienced when developing Transformational games.

- **High-Level Purpose:** The big-picture goal that is motivating your game's development
- **Audience & Context:** A deep look at the usage ecosystem for the game, beyond traditional target player demographics
- **Player Transformations:** The most important ways you want your players to be different after playing your game
- **Barriers:** An understanding of those things that stand in the way of your purpose and how you want to change your players
- **Domain Concepts:** The facts, procedures, stories, etc., that your game experience needs to embody in order to change your players
- **Expert Resources:** The people, books, etc., that you consider authoritative sources of insight and feedback on your domain
- **Prior Works:** The case studies and research that you are using as references for your transformational design strategy
- **Assessment Plan:** How you and others will decide if your game is effective

The pieces of the Framework are interconnected.

Although presented here in a specific order, developing your Transformational Framework is not a linear endeavor. The parts of the Framework inform each other, so plan on revisiting pieces throughout your process.

Think of the Transformational Framework as an outline for your team to fill in.

This book covers the Transformational Framework as a general process for any Transformational game. Use it as a guide to create a tailored transformational framework for your specific game. In this book, "the Framework" refers to the process itself, while "your framework" refers to your results of undertaking the process.

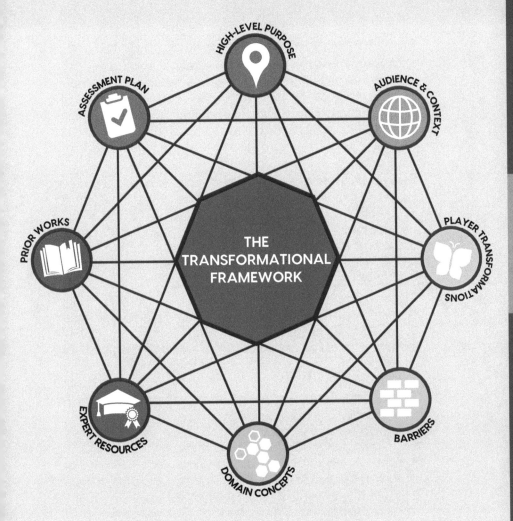

THE
TRANSFORMATIONAL
FRAMEWORK

HIGH-LEVEL PURPOSE

ASSESSMENT PLAN

AUDIENCE & CONTEXT

PRIOR WORKS

PLAYER TRANSFORMATIONS

EXPERT RESOURCES

DOMAIN CONCEPTS

BARRIERS

Tips for Using the Framework

- 1 -

Read through the full Framework guide before starting. There are eight interconnected pieces to the Framework that inform each other. You often can't talk about one piece without referring to another. Additionally, the closing chapter on production considerations for Transformational games is also quite important to read and digest.

- 2 -

Buy-in matters. Your Framework should reflect a shared vision between everyone working on the game. It will take time to complete and will work best when you are able to bring all decision-making stakeholders into the process. Before doing so, spend time explaining what the Transformational Framework is and why it is valuable. (Hopefully you can use this book as one tool for this purpose.)

If team members or partners join your project later in development, after your framework is complete, getting their buy-in still matters. Make sure you share your framework with them and take time to address their questions or suggestions.

- 3 -

Tackle the Framework as early as possible. The best time to undertake the Framework process is in pre-production before you've made many decisions. Everything from platform to art needs, and especially the game design, should be informed by your transformational framework. If you are already in the middle of development, it's not too late to benefit from the Framework, although the process will likely challenge some of the assumptions and decisions you've made so far.

- 4 -

The Framework is a tool to augment your pre-production – not replace it. Other standard pre-production tasks also still apply, such as proving out your tech pipeline, building gameplay prototypes, establishing your art style, creating a solid production schedule, etc.

- 5 -

Document your Framework. Although a written document is not the primary goal of the Transformational Framework process, **do** document your framework. There is significant value in the process itself, and you will find that you and your team internalize much of what you decide and discover along the way. But it is also beneficial to document your decisions and discoveries – for your future self to refer back to throughout development and evaluate your success, and also so that new team members or outsiders can understand what guided your design.

- 6 -

Keep your Framework in mind throughout production. The Framework process is most directly useful in pre-production when many of your foundational design decisions are being made. However, it continues to be applicable throughout production. It is a lens you should use to make decisions on everything from what features to cut to the kind of feedback to give to players during gameplay.

- 7 -

Be flexible when working through the Framework. The Framework pieces are presented in a specific order, but you may find that a different order works for you. It is also normal to revisit pieces as you establish your Framework. If you find your team is stuck on a piece, consider jumping to a different one. For each project, you will find some pieces are more important or take more time, while other pieces may be less relevant or can be addressed very quickly.

- 8 -

Your framework is not an end unto itself. The questions you will explore as part of the Transformational Framework can be challenging. Don't expect to reach perfect answers in which you are 100% confident. You may find yourself needing to move forward with development while unknowns and uncertainties still remain. That is OK. Sometimes you are not looking for a "right" answer, but **your** answer – one that will help you and your team move forward with aligned vision and purpose. And remember, you are not chained to the decisions you make in pre-production.

The Framework's Evolution

In 2011, Schell Games started its first big Transformational game with Yale University's play2PREVENT® lab: *PlayForward®*, a game to reduce HIV exposure in teens by reducing their risky behavior. We started this project at Schell as we often did – with quick protoyping. But we soon realized that the visions of our development team and client partners were misaligned. We took a step back and spent some time trying to create a better shared definition of the problem we were trying to solve. We created 'playbooks' with Yale for each high-level skill or behavior we were trying to change. Each of these playbooks outlined our shared understanding of that behavior, our theory of how to change it, and how the game would implement that theory. These documents were the forerunners of the Transformational Framework.

That experience awoke a realization in me that we needed to develop a strategic approach to the Schell Games studio process for these kinds of games. I took what we'd learned from *PlayForward* and created a template called "Transformational Goals" to be used on the next Transformational project. It only had a few pieces of the eventual Framework – purpose, transformational goals, and supporting research.

The next project happened to be *World of Lexica*, an ambitious tablet game with the goal to encourage lifelong reading in middle-schoolers. The game had already been in development for a year, but there was a general feeling on the team that they didn't understand how the game they were building would achieve the intended transformational effect. So, even though the project was well underway, we decided to try out our new Transformational Goals process. We enlisted our client as a partner in this process, and the time we all spent in this design process strengthened the final game.

This first application of this process within Schell Games was a great learning experience. We gathered up a long list of "big questions" that we felt it would be important for our development team and our client to answer.

From these questions emerged additional pieces of the Framework: the concept of barriers and the idea of more extensively defining the audience and context of the game, as well as assessment planning and strategies for incorporating expert resources and prior works.

After *Lexica*, I continued to experiment with applying this process to game projects. It made pitches clearer and production goals easier to define. These experiences convinced me that a templated process like this was extremely beneficial to Transformational game projects and something that should be done early in a project's life cycle, before big design decisions are made. It was at this point that the name "Transformational Framework" started to stick.

In 2014, I started an outline of a guide that eventually led to this book. My goal was to share the Framework in an instructional way with a wider audience of developers so that it could continue to evolve. I wanted to include not just the idea of the Framework pieces, but also supportive insights, strategies, and vocabulary to help teams work through the Framework.

To that end, I enlisted another ongoing project at Schell Games, *Happy Atoms*, to try using the Framework and this guide in their development. The *Happy Atoms* project director, Yotam Haimberg, embraced the Framework. He and his team provided feedback regularly about their experience. It was from this feedback that the last piece of the Framework was added – Key Concepts, which later become Domain Concepts.

Since then, other projects at Schell Games have used the Framework and evolving drafts of this book as an aide for their pre-production process. It has also been applied at Carnegie Mellon's Entertainment Technology Center for graduate work on a number of Transformational games.

The Framework pieces themselves have stayed fairly steady since 2015, but the book has grown significantly beyond what I initially imagined. It's exciting to be able to share it with more teams and support the world-changing potential of Transformational games.

Sabrina Culyba
Author

49

Question
#1

Why is it important that your game transform players?

High-Level Purpose

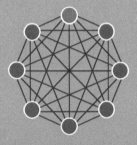

Why is it important that your game transform players?

There are a number of desired outcomes that tend to drive game development: creative expression, profit, and acclaim are all common motivators for entertainment games. Most games hope to accomplish one or more of these outcomes. Transformational games add another – player transformation. 'Add' is truly the right word because many Transformational games are also trying to make money, get recognized, or fulfill an artistic vision.

Transforming players is hard. You and your team should have a clear, shared understanding of the big-picture impact you are trying to achieve with your game by transforming players. This is your **High-Level Purpose**.

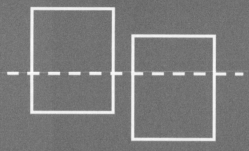

Alignment

Inspiration

Direction

The Importance of Purpose

A clear purpose provides several benefits for your team.

Agreeing on your purpose is an important early exercise in aligning vision in your team. In order to effectively use your purpose for design decisions, you will need agreement on the purpose within your team and among your key stakeholders. Ideally, everyone who will have influence over the design direction of your project should be able to quickly state the High-Level Purpose.

A purpose provides inspiration for the hard work of developing a Transformational game. Generally, humans like to feel like their work and struggle is meaningful. And it is very likely that your team will, at times, struggle. Making games is hard. Making a Transformational game is even harder. To persevere through these struggles, it will help your team to have a shared sense of why their work matters. The High-Level Purpose should evoke this value.

Your purpose is a directional compass for your design decisions. Everything else about the game, including all the other pieces of your Transformational Framework may shift as your process unfolds and you continue to refine your approach. But your High-Level Purpose should remain consistent as the true north for where you are headed with your impact.

Direction and alignment help keep your team moving together toward the right goal, while inspiration helps provide momentum.

A Good Purpose Is

- Focused on Impact, Not Product
- Concise & Memorable
- Supports Alignment for Your Team

Establishing
Your Purpose

To establish your high-level purpose, gather your team and any other key stakeholders to discuss the big-picture impact you want your Transformational game to have. Ask yourselves: *Why is it important that our game transform players?* If you are working with a client or partner that has a vision statement or mission statement, consider this as a starting point for your purpose.

Focus on the meaningful impact you want to make, not on the game. Remember, in most cases your purpose is independent of the fact that you are making a game. A game is a medium, a tool, a strategy, a means to an end – that end is your purpose. Your purpose is not about the experience you are making – it is about why you are making that experience. If you find yourself writing a purpose that starts with "Make a game that...", try cutting that first part completely and focusing on what comes after.

Make your purpose memorable. Everyone on the team should be able to quickly recite your purpose. To this end, keep your purpose concise. Consider placing it prominently in your design documents and presentations so that everyone is constantly reminded why you are making your game. This helps the purpose continue to inspire your team and keep everyone aligned on the common goal.

Remember that your purpose is for *your* team. Spend time getting the wording right for your team and stakeholders. Once you reach a place where it feels like everyone can repeat and nod along with your purpose statement, you've reached alignment. Do not get too bogged down in making it self-explanatory to all outsiders.

A clear, memorable purpose will help your entire team better contribute to the rest of the Framework process as well as the actual design and development of your game.

Three Purpose Examples

These are high-level purpose statements used by the teams of Transformational games developed at Schell Games.

PlayForward®: Elm City Stories (2012)
Purpose: Reduce HIV Exposure in At-risk Teens

Schell Games worked on *PlayForward* in partnership with Yale School of Medicine's play2PREVENT® Lab and Digitalmill. Yale came to the project with the goal of showing that a game could be used to reduce HIV exposure in at-risk teens. This big-picture intent continued to be the primary guidepost for the motivation for the project, even as the team delved deeply into the specific behavior changes the game would try to engender in players.

The World of Lexica (2015)
Purpose: Create Life-long Readers

Lexica was developed by Schell Games as part of a tablet-based curriculum initiative by Amplify. It was an expansive RPG-style tablet game that featured many books and minigames about reading skills. Though books and literacy were part of the game's early concept, when the team pushed on the inspirational *why* of the Transformational nature of the game, the purpose of instilling in players a life-long identity as a "reader" came to light.

Happy Atoms (2016)
Purpose: Demystify Chemistry

Long before *Happy Atoms* existed as a digital game, it started as a physical prototype of a new kind of molecule building set that was the brainchild of Jesse Schell, CEO of Schell Games. Jesse believed that there must be some way to make chemistry less mysterious and more intuitive for learners. This goal to demystify chemistry became the development team's high-level purpose.

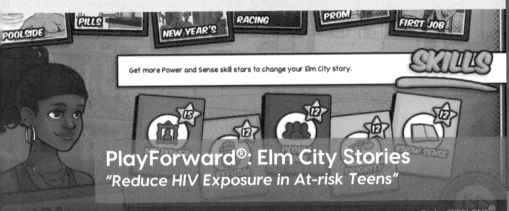

PlayForward®: Elm City Stories
"Reduce HIV Exposure in At-risk Teens"

© play2PREVENT®

The World of Lexica
"Create Lifelong Readers"

Andee's Lab

Happy Atoms
"Demystify Chemistry"

A Purpose
Is Not Enough

Many teams working on Transformational games mistake knowing their purpose for understanding their design problem.

Here is a typical scenario.

Client: We want to make a game that helps kids learn physics.

Team: Okay, a physics game, right? Here is a design for a game where the puzzles are all based on real physics and you manipulate physics properties to solve the puzzles. And, this is similar to this other game that is popular with your demographic.

Client: Sounds great! Let's build it.

Both sides of this conversation have agreed on their high-level purpose – help kids learn physics – and both have failed to give attention to why kids struggle with physics or what they really mean by "learn physics".

Consequently their design concept, while featuring physics, is not built on a foundational theory of how the gameplay will successfully change players. Because they have short-circuited the important questions represented by the rest of the Framework by leaping to a solution from their purpose, the result is likely to be a game shallowly themed around physics that has little to offer in terms of deep engagement with their purpose and is not successful at changing players.

Do not design directly from your purpose. Instead, use your purpose to guide the creation of the rest of your transformational framework and use your full framework to guide your design.

Question #2

What is the ecosystem in which your game must create change?

Audience & Context

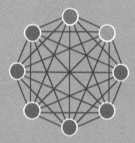

What is the ecosystem in
which your game must
create change?

Your **Audience** consists of the people you want to play, support, or use your game. This is always important to identify for a game but has additional implications for a Transformational game.

The **Context** is the environment in which your game will be played. This includes not only where, when, and how the game will be played, but also the social context of the player and other stakeholders. All of these elements can impact the effectiveness of your game.

Together the Audience and Context make up the ecosystem in which your game must create change.

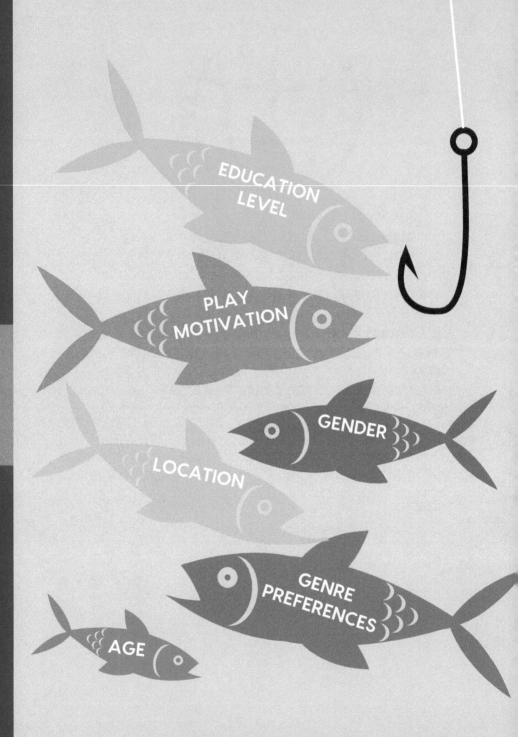

The typical game development approach to target audience focuses on understanding what will appeal to that audience based on demographic and play style factors

Target Audience
Is the Start

Defining your player audience is always important for a game. In standard game development, we usually call this the "target audience." It is typically defined primarily by:

- **Basic Demographics** such as age, gender, location, and education level
- **Play Style:** game genre preferences and play motivation

For references on play style taxonomies, see Appendix G.

Here are some examples of typical target audiences:

- 30-35 year-old women who are casual gamers
- 6-8 year-old kids who enjoy sandbox games
- 15-25 year-old hardcore male players who play competitive games
- 2-4 year-old children who play tablet games with their parents

(Note that gender tends to be simplified into genericized stereotypes of male and female when it is used for the purposes of defining the demographic of target audiences.)

Standard game development is often focused on understanding what will *appeal* to an audience.

Basic demographic stats help to guide content along axis of tone, maturity, and theme, while examining gaming style helps decide what kind of game mechanics and play patterns the target audience might expect or desire. There are (much debated) relationships between certain demographic stats and certain gaming styles. Developers sometimes first pick a demographic and then choose a game style they think will appeal to that demographic, or first come up with a game and then try to market to the demographic that they believe will enjoy the type of gameplay in their game.

Transformational games have the additional challenge of understanding how to affect *change* in the audience.

In order to do this, we have to go beyond what we normally consider critical to know about our target audience and the context that surrounds them. It's important to recognize that this is *in addition* to understanding demographics and play style, because, of course, appealing to an audience is the first step to having them play a game that might transform them.

ENTER

Understanding How to
Meet Players as They Come

START

Understanding
Transformational Gap

before   after

Comparison for
Assessing Impact

Your Audience's Initial State

The most critical additional angle to consider about your audience is their initial state – how they come to your game relative to the change you are trying to achieve. Your goal is to change players. Change necessarily implies moving from a starting condition to a new condition. How do you expect players to come to the game, in terms of your game's transformational purpose and topic?

E.g., You are designing a game to help students struggling with geometry. What is your audience's expected familiarity and skill level in geometry when they start playing your game? What can you assume they already know? What experiences, feelings, knowledge or other intersections with geometry should you expect in your audience?

Understanding initial state helps you meet your players as they are when they start your game experience. Understanding initial state helps you design for your player's entry into your game. If your game starts out assuming prior knowledge or experience that your players do not have, you may leave them behind. If your game fails to present your topic in a way that is approachable for your audience, they may decide your game is not for them.

This is highly connected to Barriers.

Initial state gives you a sense of the transformational gap your game might address. Understanding the delta between the initial state and the intended transformed state gives you a sense of how much content you will need in your game as well as how you might need to scaffold that content to help the player reach that state.

This is highly connected to Domain Concepts.

Initial state is important when assessing your game's impact. Showing change requires comparing an end state to a starting state. By exploring and documenting your audience's initial state, you create a snapshot of your audience *before* your game that can be useful for measuring impact after.

This is highly connected to Assessment.

Initial State is deeply connected to other parts of the Framework, particularly your Player Transformations, Barriers, Domain Concepts, and Assessment. You will probably need to iterate on your exploration into your audience's initial state in tandem with your development of these other Framework pieces.

External Pressures

Personal Goals

Intrinsic Interest

Your Audience's Transformational Motivation

The second critical expanded view of your audience is their transformational motivation – does your audience *want* to be transformed? Transformational motivation is distinct from play motivation. It has to do with your audience's relationship to your high-level purpose and your game's domain.

Your audience may have no transformational motivation. They may be completely disconnected or at odds with your high-level purpose. However, often there are connections such as:

- **Meeting external pressures:** There are forces outside your audience applying pressure on them to change, but your audience is not necessarily aligned with these forces.
  E.g., Earning a passing grade for a required class in which the player has little personal interest

- **Reaching personal goals:** Your audience has personal goals that are motivating them to change, though they may not be interested so much in the change itself.
  E.g., Completing training that supports the player's growth and success in their chosen profession

- **Supporting intrinsic interest & identity:** Your audience is innately interested in your game's topic, purpose, or their own transformation.
  E.g., Learning more about a subject the player self-identifies as enjoyable or meaningful to them

Understanding transformational motivation will inform how directly you can approach your high-level purpose and topic. Will your players be turned-off if they detect your intent? In this case, perhaps your game should be a "headfake" where players don't realize they are supposed to be learning or changing. Or would knowing your game's transformational intent increase your player's buy-in?

Transformational motivation helps you understand where you should focus your design. If your players are personally motivated to transform, you may invest more development effort in game structures that help them see their transformational progress (such as badges or stats.) On the other hand, if your players are not motivated by your transformational purpose, it's even more important to connect with their motivation in some other way. This often involves doubling down on fulfilling their existing play style preferences with your game's mechanics.

For more on supporting feedback for self-motivated players, see **Pg. 207**.

Socioeconomic
Status

Access

Cultural
Norms

Related
Content

Social
Connections

Formalized
Structures

Additional Components of Context

Here are some additional angles on understanding your audience based on the context that surrounds them. You may notice overlap between these concepts. This list is not meant to be exhaustive or definitive but offers lenses on the context around audiences that are valuable for your team to explore.

- **Socioeconomic Status (SES):** This includes the player's economic standing and education level. SES impacts behavior, disposition, knowledge, health, and many other aspects of life. You can also expand SES to look at the community in which the player lives, with implications for other items on this list like access and social connections.

- **Access:** What sort of technology and resources does your audience have access to? Where and when will they be able to logistically play your game? How will their access impact their ability to follow through with transformations such as behavior changes?

- **Cultural Norms:** If you are designing for a particular region or cultural group, adoption and impact of your game may depend on it fitting into the social norms of that group. "Cultural norms" refers to symbols, beliefs, language, behavioral patterns, social hierarchies, traditions, etc. This includes understanding what is taboo or offensive to your players or their communities.

- **Related Content:** What else is your audience interacting with related to your purpose? Are they taking related classes? Watching related media? How will your game fit in? How can your game complement (and be complemented by) these other experiences and resources?

- **Social Connections:** Social relationships play an important role in influencing behavior, beliefs, and identities. Take time to understand the social relationships that are important to your players so you can decide how, if at all, your game will interact with those connections. You may decide to leverage them, or find that you need to overcome them.

- **Formalized Structures:** Will your game be used within a formalized structure such as a school or community organization? How will this influence both your players' potential transformations as well as how your game is accessed or perceived? Are there rules or integration requirements you need to understand to be successful? Will a moderator such as a teacher be interacting with your players? If so, what is their role in your players' transformations or otherwise facilitating your game?

Audiences Beyond Players

Often in Transformational games there are a number of stakeholder parties who are not directly playing the game but whose voices and concerns are important to consider.

- **Parents:** If your game is targeting minors, you should consider the role of parents or other adult guardians. They may serve as gatekeepers to the game, so you may need to appeal to them in order to access your target players. In general, parents want to keep their kids safe and feel like they are successful as parents. Consider how your game could be perceived as helping or hindering these goals.
- **Client or Funders:** These are the people who commissioned your game or who support it financially. They may be genuinely invested in the transformational outcome of your game, but they may also be interested in its critical reception and financial success.
- **Researchers:** If you are working on a game in partnership with a university or through a grant funder, you may find yourself working with researchers who plan to study your game and its impact on players. Researchers are usually interested in publishing academic papers on their work.
- **Schools and School Districts:** These entities are effective gatekeepers to the classroom for many educational games. When they are determining what educational material they purchase, they are often concerned with, or beholden to, educational standards and assessments. And often those schools with the most need have the least access to funding and technology resources.
- **Teachers:** If your game is intended for use in the classroom, then you are partnering, directly or indirectly, with teachers. They have needs related to getting buy-in from their administration, integrating your game into their lesson plans, and also managing their classroom logistically.

Parents

Client or Funder

Researchers

Schools & Districts

Teachers

Parents

- **Health Safety:** My kid is going to be safe from physical and emotional harm while playing this game, right? Do I need to worry about bullying or predation by other players?
- **Moral Safety:** My kid's not going to be exposed to something I disapprove of in this game, right?
- **Guilt Free:** I'm not going to feel like a bad parent by letting my kids play this, right?
- **Vetted:** Is this game good? Show me some entity I trust and respect vouching for it.
- **Help Me:** How is this going to help me with my role as a parent?

Clients & Funders

- **Responsibility:** If those at the top of our organization knew how much this game cost to develop, would they think the money well spent?
- **PR:** Will this game show well and make us look good? We're not going to have any PR snafus with this game's content, are we?
- **Strategy:** Will this game complement our overall strategy of success? (Impact, Sales...)
- **Proof:** How can we prove the effectiveness of this game so we can make confident claims?

Researchers

- **Funding:** Will working with you on this game help me get my own research funded?
- **Data:** Will I be able to get clean data out of this game that I can use for analysis and publication?
- **Adaptability:** Will I be able to change things in the game later and then gather more data?
- **Publishing:** I must be able to publish my findings. If I work with you, are you willing to keep the data we collect out of the public sphere until I publish?

Common
Stakeholder Concerns

Schools

- **Rules Fit:** Our school has many layers of rules we must follow that control what we can use or buy. Will this game qualify?
- **Happy Parents:** When kids show their parents this game, we won't get any angry phone calls or emails, right?
- **IT Integration:** We only have brand X devices and our wi-fi is limited. Will this game work for us?
- **Easy Support:** We have limited IT staff. How easy is this game to maintain and update?
- **Standards Alignment:** Does this game meet the curriculum standards we have to follow?
- **Assessment:** Our funding is tied to our students' performance. Will this game show results that align with our student assessment goals? How easy is it to see reports of these results?

Teachers

- **Good Guidance:** I want examples on how to integrate this into my classroom. Do you have any?
- **Unlockability:** I have my own schedule and very limited classroom time. Will this game let me easily skip to particular content?
- **Classroom Management:** I need to be able to monitor and focus a group of students. What features of this game will help me with those challenges?
- **Assessment:** I need to know if my students are doing well or if they are stuck. Can the game help me measure student mastery? I also need to get data out of this game and integrated into my grading process. How easy will that be?
- **Drill Support:** Some skills I teach fundamentally require repetitious practice. Could this game make this kind of practice less boring for my students?
- **Cost Structure:** Do I need to pay per student? Is the price point high enough that I'll need to fill out paperwork to make a special purchase request?

Designing for Rural Ethiopia

> **My team and I were tasked with developing transformational games for early adolescent girls in rural Ethiopia. While we were collaborating with local experts, our game design team was not familiar with Ethiopian girl culture. That meant we needed to spend a lot of time listening before making design decisions.**

During our research phase, we discovered that girls had a culture of sharing games. Girls told us that when they went to visit family in other towns, they were obligated to teach local girls any new games that they'd learned. This was an opportunity for our games to spread naturally, and for girls to feel a sense of ownership of the games they were playing.

At the same time, this created a new problem. If we were distributing the games, we could provide any materials needed to play. If girls were teaching each other, though, game materials couldn't be centrally distributed. Girls would need to be able to share game materials with each other as peers.

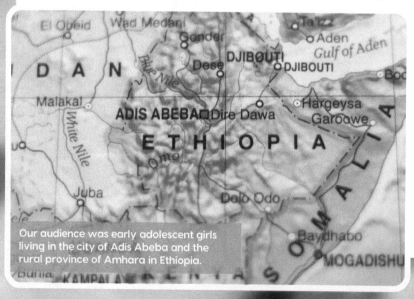

Our audience was early adolescent girls living in the city of Adis Abeba and the rural province of Amhara in Ethiopia.

Find references related for this developer story in **Appendix H.**

Taken together, these two insights changed our approach to the games we were designing. We realized that all our games needed to be playable with free, locally available materials. We observed what physical materials girls already played with, and we collaborated with girls to identify what other materials they had access to. Instead of creating beautiful physical parts for our game, we designed game pieces that could be copied by girls using seeds, string, cardboard, plastic bags, tin can lids, and flat stones.

A trio of two-sided rocks could be substituted for a 6-sided die. Girls could create these easily with found materials.

We also considered how girls might teach each other the game rules. While we produced written versions of our game rules that girls could copy, we assumed that our games would primarily be taught orally. That meant creating mnemonics and songs to go along with our written rules.

These choices wouldn't be appropriate in every context, but for the girls we were working with, shareable and reproducible games were key!

Jessica Hammer
Assistant Professor
Carnegie Mellon University

Persona Profiles

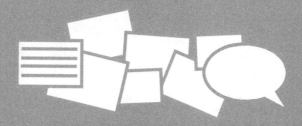

Artifacts: Photo Diaries,
Collages, etc.

Fly-on-the-Wall
Observation/Shadowing

Useful Techniques

How can you get such a broad and nuanced understanding of your player audience and the context around them? Leverage the disciplines of **Human-Centered Design (HCD)** and **Participatory Design** (also known as **Co-Design**). Both of these design approaches offer techniques to more deeply understand your audience & context. Here are just a few ideas:

Create a persona profile of a prototypical audience member.
Start by outlining the things you'd ideally know about your audience to inform your design: their goals, priorities, concerns, patterns, attitudes, etc. Identify any gaps in your knowledge. Use surveys, interviews, observations, and artifacts to address these gaps.

For references on Human-Centered Design, see Appendix I.

E.g., You are designing a game for training new city employees. You create a persona profile for a fictional "Robin Newhire," and include details (such as her prior work experience, expectations for her new job, and her home life) that reflect the majority of new hires. You help vet these details through surveys and interviews of real city employees. When making design decisions, your team considers how it would be received by Robin.

Invite your audience to create their own artifacts such as photo diaries or collages.
To capture your audience's authentic context and sense of self, ask them to create their own cultural documentation such as photo diaries, collages, or personal stories. Then ask them to tell you in their own words about what they made. Pay attention to what is important to them, what details they focus on, the words they use, and their emotional connection to each piece.

E.g., You are designing a game to promote civic engagement in high schoolers. You might ask a group of students to collect photos that capture the impact of government on themselves and their family. You could then have them present their photos and talk about them. In this way, you learn about their existing knowledge, dispositions, and relationships to government, in their own words and images.

Observe your audience in their context.
You can learn a lot by directly observing your audience in their real-word context. How do they behave? How do they talk and interact with others? What are their patterns? Where do they get stuck or have problems? What choices do they make? (Of course, don't intrude on the personal privacy of your audience without their permission!)

E.g., You are designing a game to improve communication patterns between parents and young children. You might choose to observe parent/child groups in settings such as playgrounds or restaurants.

You Are Not
Your Target Audience*

It can be tempting to make assumptions about your target audience. Sometimes these assumptions even come from relevant personal experience with that audience. But do not rely solely on these assumptions when starting your process. Too often this leads to a false sense of confidence that you understand your audience's motivations, initial state, and context. This in turn can hamper your design decisions by obscuring problems to solve or pulling your focus based on mistaken priorities.

Vet what you think you know about your audience with actual members of that audience. This is why human-centered design and participatory design are so critical to establishing a clear picture of your audience and context. These strategies bring your audience into the process so what you learn has an innate authenticity to it.

Beware of convincing yourself that you are a good enough proxy for your target audience. Invest time in clearly establishing your true target audience. Make sure to capture what sets them apart. Understanding this and believing this matters is a bulwark against the temptation to simply fall back on yourself and your team as proxies for that audience.

Invest in figuring out how to access your target audience. The temptation to rely on yourself as a proxy for the audience can be particularly great if it's difficult to access your target audience. Finding or creating a channel of access to your audience can help prevent falling into this trap.

Honestly acknowledge when you are using a proxy for your target audience. It's not realistic to have access to your authentic audience at every moment. There will certainly be moments when you'll need to make decisions or playtest your ideas without your audience. Try to stay aware of these moments and have a plan on how you'll follow up with your target audience eventually.

* Even if you *are* making a game where you are legitimately a member of the target audience, question your assumptions and seek out input from others to figure out what is unique to your personal experience and what of your personal perspective is generally shared by your audience as a whole.

Question #3

How should players be different after playing your game?

Player Transformations

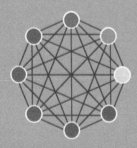

How should players be
different after playing
your game?

The heart of transformational success is how your game changes players.

If your high-level purpose is your inspirational *why*, your **Player Transformations** are your focused *what*. They outline the specific ways you intend your player to be changed by your game experience in order to achieve your purpose.

It's important to recognize that transformation isn't just about players learning new facts or skills. There are many other ways to transform players and often, to meet your purpose, your game must change players along several different axes.

Player transformations, in outlining the specific intended impact of your game, also provide a beginning blueprint for how you will assess your game and determine your transformational success.

**Describe Player Change
From Initial State**

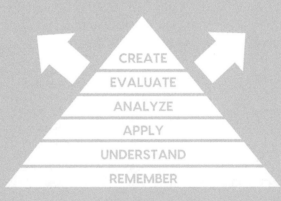

CREATE
EVALUATE
ANALYZE
APPLY
UNDERSTAND
REMEMBER

**Expand Beyond
Learning Objectives**

What Are Player Transformations?

Like your high-level purpose, player transformations are independent of the fact that you are making a game. They are not about what the player will do in the game. They are the specific ways the player will be changed by your game that will transfer and persist beyond the game experience.

Player Transformations describe changes from your player's initial state. As we covered in the previous chapter, the player's initial state is how they come to your game – what they already know, think, feel, do, etc. Player transformations implicitly build from this initial state.

Player Transformations are an expanded form of learning objectives. If you are familiar with education or educational games, you've probably heard the terms learning objectives or learning goals.

Learning objectives are often based on Bloom's Taxonomy, which describes a hierarchal progression of six levels of skills that represent learning: Remembering, Understanding, Applying, Analyzing, Evaluating, and Creating. Bloom's Taxonomy is a powerful tool for describing a player's mastery of solicited performance of a skill or area of knowledge. Becoming familiar with Bloom's Taxonomy is very valuable for working in education and for working with specific types of player transformations. Good learning objectives, like good player transformations, are specific, measurable, and player-centered. However, Bloom's Taxonomy doesn't directly represent a number of other ways we can change players, such as behavior, choices, feelings, sense of identity, or physical changes.

For references on Bloom's Taxonomy, see Appendix J.

Ultimately, "learning" is not always sufficient to describe the ways we want to change players and may bias our focus towards mastery of facts and skills, when transformations can cover a much broader spectrum of impact.

Types of Transformation

Player Transformation is multifaceted and can cover a broad spectrum of impact on players.
Teams starting out on Transformational games tend to focus primarily on the knowledge and skill aspects of player change. These are the types of transformations that usually fall within traditional learning objectives:

- **Knowledge:** The player knows something new.
  E.g., Player can recall the meaning of vocabulary words
- **Skill:** The player can do something new.
  E.g., Player can solve algebraic equations

However, changing humans often means changing more than what they know or can do. Here are a number of other broad categories of transformation that are worth considering for your game:

- **Physical:** The player's body is changed.
  E.g., Player has a lower resting heart rate
- **Disposition:** The player's feelings are changed.
  E.g., Player feels more positively about people of non-binary gender identities
- **Experience:** The player's personal anecdotes are changed.
  E.g., Player has experienced what it's like to deal with discrimination based on skin color
- **Behavior:** The player acts in a new way.
  E.g., Player chooses healthier foods to eat
- **Belief:** The player's sense of truth is changed.
  E.g., Player believes that human trafficking is a big problem worth tackling with urgency
- **Relationships:** The player's social relationships are changed.
  E.g., Player has more trust in community police
- **Identity:** The player's sense of self is changed.
  E.g., Player starts to describe themselves as "artistic"
- **Society:** The world around the player is changed.
  E.g., The overall voter turnout increases in a community

This list is not mean to be exhaustive or definitive. Divisions between the types here are debatable. The purpose of these categories of transformation is to initiate conversation about the specific and varied ways players can be transformed. Use this list to help your team think about how you want to transform your own players in a more nuanced way.

KNOWLEDGE
the player knows something new

Facts
Information
Recall

SKILL
the player can do something new

Abilities
Technique
Application
Dexterity

PHYSICAL
the player's body is changed

Health
Biometrics
Performance

DISPOSITION
the player's feelings are changed

Attitudes
Feelings
Motivations

EXPERIENCE
the player's personal story is changed

Exposure
Perspective
Reference Point
Familiarity

BEHAVIOR
the player acts in a different way

Habits
Actions
Choices

BELIEF
the player's sense of truth is altered

Perceptions
Worldview
Opinion

RELATIONSHIPS
the player's social interactions are changed

Connections
Communication
Status

IDENTITY
the player's sense of self is changed

Labels
Associations
Values

SOCIETY
the world around the player is changed

Community
Environment
Culture

Strategies for Approaching
Your Purpose

Guidance
for Assessment

Why Transformations Matter

If your true "goal" is your high-level purpose, why do you need player transformations?

Player transformations outline your specific strategy for pursuing your high-level purpose. While your high-level purpose should be inspirational, this often means it's not very practical. Although it can motivate your team, it likely won't provide much in the way of concrete guidance for what to build. There are likely to be many potential ways you could approach any given high-level purpose. Player transformations become your game's specific approach and provide much more targeted guidance on the impact your game plans to make on players, which in turn informs the implementation and content for your game.

Player transformations are a blueprint to help you and others define how to assess the transformational success of your game. They are fundamentally tied to the evaluation of your game as Transformational. As they describe how you intend your players to be different after they play your game, they can be used to drive the design of assessments to measure these changes.

Transformations with Happy Atoms

Happy Atoms began as a concept for a new type of molecular modeling system – one where magnetic connections would give kids an intuitive sense of how atoms bond together and where computer vision technology would enable first-hand exploration of the molecular world without any prior knowledge about chemistry. This big picture vision drove the definition of our high-level purpose: Demystify Chemistry.

Happy Atoms combined a physical modeling system with a digital game to enable players to explore the world of molecular chemistry.

When we first set out to define our player transformations, knowledge transformations were the obvious choice because the experience we were making was about chemistry and science – that's about facts, right? There was a desire to stuff the experience with information that players would be able to recite after playing the game. What the Transformational Framework did, particularly the list of transformation types, was give our team the language to consider other approaches. Knowledge was important, but it wasn't really the heart of what we were trying to do. Realizing this allowed us to de-emphasize knowledge to elevate a different angle on transformation – Belief.

This shift created a sense of ownership of our transformation that led to the team opening up to changing their own beliefs about chemistry. I had a background in chemistry but most of the rest of team had stories of their own struggles with chemistry from grade school. We cultivated a culture where we all tried to leave negative associations or insecurities with chemistry behind and simply be open to curiosity about how chemistry permeated the world around us. Members of the team would bring up questions like "Why does water remove some stains but not others?" I would try to explain or find the answer. This curiosity-driven attitude shift on our team was exactly what we realized we needed to create for our players.

Find references for this developer story in Appendix K.

Many people go into chemistry assuming it's mostly about math, because it's often taught with an emphasis on calculations. And not many kids learn chemistry early enough to see it as a base worldview on how things work. Instead we tend to adopt physical processes or biological processes as our core model of what drives phenomenon around us. Chemistry is so much about what you can't see. We realized our approach had to be reintroducing chemistry as something entirely new to discover that would circumvent players' existing biases against chemistry and would change their underlying assumptions about how the world works.

We debated for a bit on if our primary transformation should be one of identity. Were we trying to get players to see themselves more as someone who found chemistry to be approachable? Asking these questions helped us focus further. We weren't trying to change kids so that they liked chemistry more necessarily (though we suspected that would come along naturally). We wanted players to understand how chemistry permeates the world around them. So our transformation was less about "who am I" and more about "how do I see the world."

Player transformations gave us the language we needed to talk about how we wanted to make Happy Atoms. It allowed us to be more intentional in our approach by giving us a way to break down how we wanted to change players to really understand our shared transformational goals as a team. Ultimately our primary belief transformations became one of three experience pillars during development – one that is a direct answer to our high-level purpose:

Demystify chemistry by cultivating curiosity!

Happy Atoms was supported in part by the Institute of Education Sciences, U.S. Department of Education, through the Small Business Innovation Research (SBIR) program contract ED-IES-15-C-0025 to Schell Games.

Cultivate Curiosity

Why doesn't the atmosphere

Our belief transformation eventually led to one of our core experience pillars: Cultivate Curiosity.

Yotam Haimberg
Project Director, Happy Atoms

1. Imagine Player Impact On Purpose

2. Focus on a Central Transformation

3. Define Supporting Transformations

Choosing Player Transformations

How do you get from your high-level purpose to a list of player transformations? Here are some key questions to ask:

- **What central change in individual players would impact your purpose in a significant way?** This question will probably lead you to a central transformation of a type that tends toward something externally observable, such as a skill change, behavior change, or physical change.
  E.g., Your high-level purpose is to improve urban air quality. You consider what specific changes in individual players could impact air quality. Based on your audience and expert input, you decide to focus on players reducing usage of personal automobiles.

- **Can your central change be made more specific in strategy?** Sometimes your first pass on a central player change is quite broad in terms of how it might manifest. Leverage the other aspects of your Transformational Framework to help you focus your approach.
  E.g., Continuing the urban air quality game example, you realize there are lots of approaches to reducing personal automobile usage – car pooling, public transit, etc. You decide to focus on increasing player usage of bikes in place of cars. This decision is informed by your subject-matter experts and looking at other complementary initiatives undertaken in many cities.

  The best Framework tools for this are: Audience & Context, **Expert Resources, Prior Works,** and Domain Concepts.

- **What are the underlying player transformations that contribute to the central change?** Usually, your central player transformation is dependent on other connected transformations. A behavior may be dependent on knowledge or identity. A relationship may be dependent on belief and disposition. A skill may be dependent on knowledge and experience. Again, you will use the pieces of the Transformational Framework to help reveal these important transformation connections and help you decide which are the most important to include in the list of transformations you will pursue.
  E.g., For your urban air quality game, your supporting transformations include players being able to perform basic bike maintenance, players demonstrating basic bike safety while riding, players self-identifying as someone who would commute by bike, and players understanding the positive impact biking has on themselves and their community.

  The best Framework tools for this are: Barriers and **Prior Works** (specifically research).

A Good Transformation Is

- Centered on the Player
- Assessable & Achievable
- Framed Against Initial State

Writing Your Player Transformations

Like any piece of your Framework, you'll want to iterate on your player transformations so that they are as useful to your team as possible. Here are some general guidelines on writing good player transformations:

Clearly center your player transformations on the player. Include the player as the subject of each statement. Avoid referencing your game or the player's actions in the game as part of your player transformations. Be specific about the verb that represents your targeted change in the player after the game is over. Beware of relying on generic verbs like "know" or "learn."

> **Before:** Learn how to change a bike tire.
> **After:** The player can successfully change a bike tire.

Make sure your player transformations feel assessable and achievable. These statements are how you and others will measure your game's transformational success, so make sure it seems plausible that you could achieve them. If a particular transformation seems like a stretch to achieve, considering either cutting it or looking for a more approachable underlying transformation to target instead.

As you decide on the wording for your transformations, consider how you would assess each transformation. You don't need to be so specific as to enumerate content in each statement, but you do want to imply a realistic scope of change.

> **Before:** The player knows Spanish.
> **After:** The player can introduce themselves in spoken Spanish.

Frame your player transformations in contrast to your audience's initial state. Remember, change is relative. Revisit your audience's initial state and consider including words like "more", "less", "increased", or "decreased" to acknowledge that your game's impact may be more about moving the needle on a player change than absolutely defining the player's post-game state.

> **Before:** The player loves reading.
> **After:** The player has increased positive feelings about reading.

Losing Sight
of the Obvious

It might seem obvious to state that player transformation is the goal of a Transformational game. And yet, even teams who agree with this statement often end up neglecting the transformational aspects of their game development while focusing on the engagement aspects. Why? Because engagement is something that game developers and the game industry are used to iterating on and optimizing for.

Transforming players is a new, additional way to think about success. Without intentional effort, developers focus on what they already know. Additionally, engagement is something developers understand how to observe during gameplay and through analytics. It is usually more straightforward to measure if players like your game or how far they got in your game than to measure how they have been changed by your game in ways that extend beyond their play experience.

Here are a couple of ways this can manifest:

Your iteration focuses primarily on understanding and meeting engagement feedback, rather than transformational feedback. Like every part of your game, its transformational impact will need iteration. You won't get it right the first time. If you aren't playtesting and iterating on how your game transforms your players, you probably aren't owning the sentiment that transformation is the goal.

Transformational success is discussed primarily as a factor of how players complete the game. Players completing your game is not necessarily a sign of transformation. If your approach to evaluating your transformational success is primarily player progress in your game, you probably aren't spending enough time thinking specifically about how the player themselves will be transformed.

Your goal is not to make a game, it's to transform players – your game is the medium you are using to achieve this goal.

Question #4

Why aren't your players already transformed?

Barriers

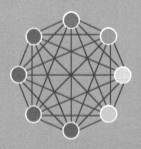

Why aren't your
players already
transformed?

The way you frame and understand a problem strongly influences the answers you reach. So it's important to step back and make sure you understand what problem you are really trying to solve.

Barriers are that real problem. They are what stands in the way of your players' transformation and the achievement of your High-Level Purpose.

Understanding your barriers will help to focus your design strategy for your Transformational game.

Initial
Player State

Barriers

Transformed
Player State

The Barriers
Are the Way

Barriers are things that prevent or hinder your audience's transformation and the achievement of your high-level purpose. They are tightly informed by a deep understanding of the audience and context. Another related term sometimes used in design circles is **pain points**.

Here are a few hypothetical examples:

- In making a game for teachers to use in 10th grade chemistry classrooms to impact student engagement in related careers, you discover that one barrier is that many students are 2 or more years behind in their math skills and so struggle with any chemistry activities that involve math. You might decide that addressing this barrier of math is just as important (if not more) as directly addressing attitudes around chemistry.

- In making a game to impact the spread of an STD in teens, you discover one barrier is that your audience has misconceptions about how prevalent this STD is in their peer group and so underestimates their own risk.

- In making a game to improve the eating habits of a particular population, you discover that this population tends to live in communities with no nearby grocery store and therefore limited access to fresh fruits and vegetables. This is a barrier that will hinder your player's eating habits, even if your game teaches them about nutrition or motivates them to eat well. Can your game help your players in the face of this barrier?

Each of these barriers reflects something that stands between who your players are when they encounter your game and who you want them to be after the game experience is over. **The path from the player's initial state to their transformed state goes through your barriers.**

Opportunities
for Impact

Gameplay Idea
Catalysts

Why
Barriers Matter

Barriers illuminate the problems your game design should potentially target to support your players' transformation.

Barriers identify gaps in existing support for your purpose where there is opportunity for your game to create impact. By articulating these barriers, you can then discuss the effect those barriers have on your player's transformational potential and how your game will (or won't) try to impact that effect. This is not just about understanding what the most prominent barriers are; it is also about considering what your game can effectively address. Deciding *not* to address a barrier can be just as empowering as deciding to address one. By limiting your focus, you can leverage your time and resources to make a stronger impact on a few barriers, rather than being stretched thin by trying to address them all.

Barriers are catalysts for gameplay ideas because they highlight problems and conflicts related to your purpose. These problems and conflicts can create a strong basis for game mechanics and narrative. Think through what would have to change about your audience, or the world around your audience, for a barrier to be overcome. Then consider how the game could support or represent that same change through mechanics.

E.g., You want to tackle the barrier of access to grocery stores in the example of the nutrition game mentioned on the last page. One strategy might be to include a system in the game that helps players gain knowledge of which healthy foods last the longest under which conditions even if their shopping trips are infrequent due to access. This could help your audience choose these foods during their own real-world shopping trips. Another strategy could be to introduce the player to fresh foods that are relatively easy to grow in containers at home. And a still different strategy could be educating players on how to advocate for better public transit or city planning in their community to make grocery access more equitable.

Barriers sit at the intersection of the real-world struggle for your purpose and the potential impact of your game mechanics. Because of this, iterating on your barriers will typically correspond with iteration on your player transformations.

Types of Barriers

Your barriers will be largely unique to your purpose, player transformations, and audience. However, there are common themes that arise across even very different projects. Here is a list of barrier "types" to consider for your game:

- **Motivation:** It doesn't align strongly to your audience's wants or needs
  E.g., lack of interest could be a barrier in understanding of history events

- **Relevance:** It seems distant or disconnected from your audience
  E.g., distance from the impact of a social justice issue could be a barrier in generating activism

- **Social Norms:** Your audience has taboos or biases that interfere with their transformation
  E.g., social norms about gender roles can be a barrier to equal rights for women in some cultures

- **Access:** Your audience lacks resources or is blocked from resources that are needed to be transformed
  E.g., lack of regular access to healthcare could be a barrier to improving patient self-advocacy skills

- **Ability:** It requires practiced skill your audience lacks
  E.g., pronunciation of unfamiliar speech sounds can be a barrier to foreign language fluency

- **Complexity:** It overwhelms your audience in its scope
  E.g., the complex nature of medical surgeries could be a barrier to preventing errors that impact patient safety

- **Unfamiliarity:** Your audience isn't aware of something or only minimally aware of it
  E.g., the invisible nature of atoms could be a barrier to understanding chemistry

- **Misconceptions:** Your audience actively believes something that isn't true
  E.g., misconceptions about what items can be recycled could be a barrier to effective recycling in a community

- **Fear:** There's a (perceived or actual) risk or danger that prevents your audience from being transformed
  E.g., apprehension about a positive diagnosis could be a barrier to improving STD testing rates

This list of barrier types is not meant to be exhaustive and definitive, but it is a useful starting point. It can be a helpful exercise to run through this list while thinking about your high-level purpose and your audience & context.

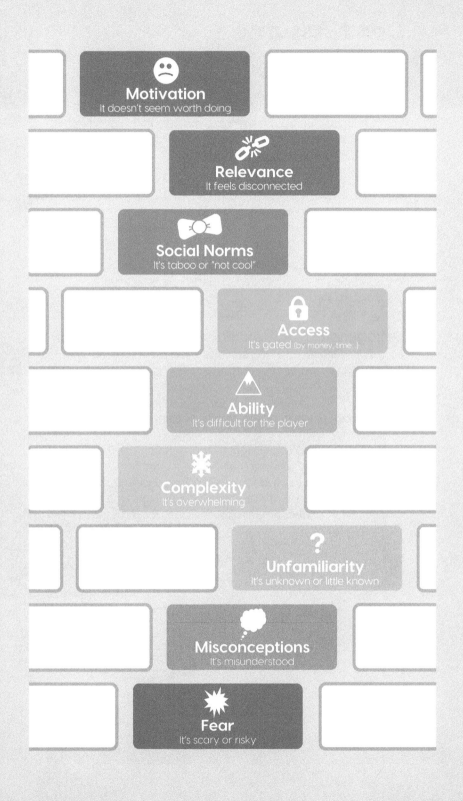

Motivation
It doesn't seem worth doing

Relevance
It feels disconnected

Social Norms
It's taboo or "not cool"

Access
It's gated (by money, time...)

Ability
It's difficult for the player

Complexity
It's overwhelming

Unfamiliarity
It's unknown or little known

Misconceptions
It's misunderstood

Fear
It's scary or risky

Don't Assume You Know

There is a natural inclination to start coming up with a list of barriers based on your existing understanding of the problem. This is a fine starting point. It can serve to document your own assumptions. But the real work of barriers involves going beyond your existing knowledge by reaching beyond yourself.

Pursue expertise and research. Draw on subject-matter resources, including your client and other experts. Look for existing academic research on the barriers to your purpose that exist for your audience.

During this process, **use the list of barrier types as keywords** in discussions and searches. For example, researching "misconceptions reading" will help find sources that talk about misconceptions that hinder reading or learning to read.

Engage with your audience. Barriers are often tightly connected to aspects of your audience & context. As with defining your audience, you can use human-centered design and participatory design strategies to learn more about your audience:

For references on Human-centered Design, see Appendix I.

- **Observe them in a real-world setting** to witness barriers firsthand.
- **Hold a focus group** to talk to them directly and understand what barriers they themselves have identified.
- **Involve them in co-design exercises** and, in doing so, learn what barriers they prioritize in their designs and how they approach addressing them.

As you explore barriers, be open to the unexpected. Sometimes the most important barriers are also the most surprising.

The World of Lexica was an RPG-style tablet-based game developed by Schell Games in 2015 in partnership with Amplify, with a high-level purpose of turning middle schoolers into lifelong readers. To really understand the problem, we had to turn it around with a powerful word – why? Why do some kids not read that much? We had to become curious about the problem.

Getting kids to read is a persistent problem in education and most persistent problems are more complex than they initially appear. Digging into the research about why kids don't read revealed a lengthy list of barriers. What was interesting was some of the most important barriers were not ones that we had naively considered to be part of the problem. Most people on the team had assumed that reading was not cool and that kids today had so many more options that they would rather do other things like play games. So, we just had to use our game to show them that reading was cool.

But one of the biggest barriers was simply access to books. Another high-impact barrier was time available for voluntary reading and it tied closely into another important barrier: exposure to a variety of books allowing kids to find at least one book or genre that they enjoyed. These three barriers ended up influencing the play pattern we designed. The game was broken into episodes that would be released gradually by players' schools. Each episode introduced the player to characters and passages from a variety of books. Since the game was bundled with an e-book reader and free books, the design intent was that the time between episodes left space for players to check out any books from that episode that had piqued their interest. Additional gameplay features also provided light bonuses to players for their reading exploration.

Altogether we identified 13 barriers. We didn't address all of them directly in our design, but our awareness of them definitely influenced our direction and decisions.

Sabrina Culyba
Transformational Designer
The World of Lexica

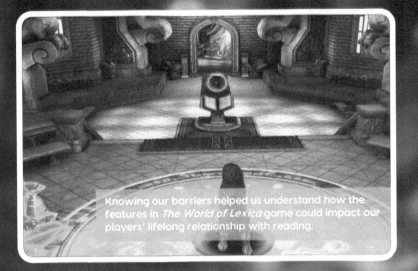

Knowing our barriers helped us understand how the features in *The World of Lexica* game could impact our players' lifelong relationship with reading.

The World of Lexica - Identified Barriers

- Weak technical reading skills such as syntax, vocabulary, fluency
- Not given enough time for voluntary reading
- Do not know a book (or type of books) that is personally enjoyable/meaningful
- Have never experienced "Reading flow"
- Lack prior knowledge and context to understand value/enjoy certain books
- Don't believe reading to be relevant to them
- Lack confidence (feelings of self-efficacy) about reading
- Do not see themselves as "readers"
- Believe they cannot get better at reading or cannot become a "reader"
- Have negative social norm perceptions about reading: No one does it; Not cool; Boring
- Lack access to reading material, particularly books
- Other things demand their attention more than reading
- Have had a negative experience with reading such as non-autonomous reading with heavy emphasis on worksheets, essays, etc.; or lack of permission to abandon a book that is not enjoyable

Find references for this
developer story in Appendix L.

**Attack
Directly**

**Scaffold Over
Or Around**

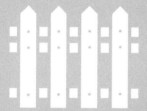

**Constrain
Your Audience**

**Acknowledge
But Set Aside**

Choosing Your Barrier Battles

You may identify more barriers than you can fully address within the scope of your game. That is OK. Not all barriers make sense to try to address directly through your game, though all barriers are worth knowing. Even if you could address every barrier, you have limited resources during game development that will require you to be selective. For each barrier that you identify, decide if:

Your game will address it, by...

- **Trying to eliminate it**
  E.g., The barrier is a misconception – your game prominently features and dispels this misconception

- **Trying to scaffold over or around it**
  E.g., The barrier is a cultural norm which makes talking about your topic taboo – your game uses a metaphor and fantasy theming to avoid triggering these feelings of breaking a taboo

Your game won't address it, by...

- **Using it to constrain your audience further**
  E.g., The barrier is access to resources – you decide that although some of your initial target audience may not have access, you still feel like you can best make progress towards your purpose by accepting that your audience will be limited to those with access

- **Acknowledging it but focusing on other barriers**
  E.g., The barrier is unfamiliarity with subject-matter information. You decide focusing on this barrier is not in-scope for your team, instead allowing that structures outside your game (such as classroom instruction) will need to address this barrier while your game supports other barriers such as motivation.

Through discussion with stakeholders and subject-matter experts, and research into your audience, prioritize the barriers and pick a subset to focus on in your game. To do this, balance which barriers feel most important to tackle for your audience with how well you can address these barriers through the medium of a game. You may identify multiple barriers for one player transformation or a barrier that impacts multiple transformations. Exploring barriers may very likely even lead you to revisit your list of player transformations.

Question

#5

What is essential to include in the game to transform your players?

Domain
Concepts

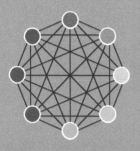

What is essential to include in the game to transform your players?

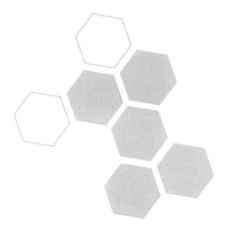

Transformational games typically deal with specific subjects, such as "algebra" or "history" or "racism." We call this the *domain* of the game. Most domains are too broad or deep to fully encapsulate in a single game. Just knowing the domain doesn't offer much guidance on what actually needs to be in your game.

Any domain can be broken down into sub-domains, but what is really helpful is to drill more granularly into your **Domain Concepts.** These are individual facts, narratives, processes, terms, etc. that are contained within your domain. Domain concepts often become the basis for a Transformational game's content and mechanics.

There is a relationship between the number and complexity of concepts you want to include in your game and the scope of game necessary to present those concepts. Creating a mapping of your domain concepts allows you to specify the bits of your domain that you believe must be embodied in some way in the game in order to achieve your player transformations.

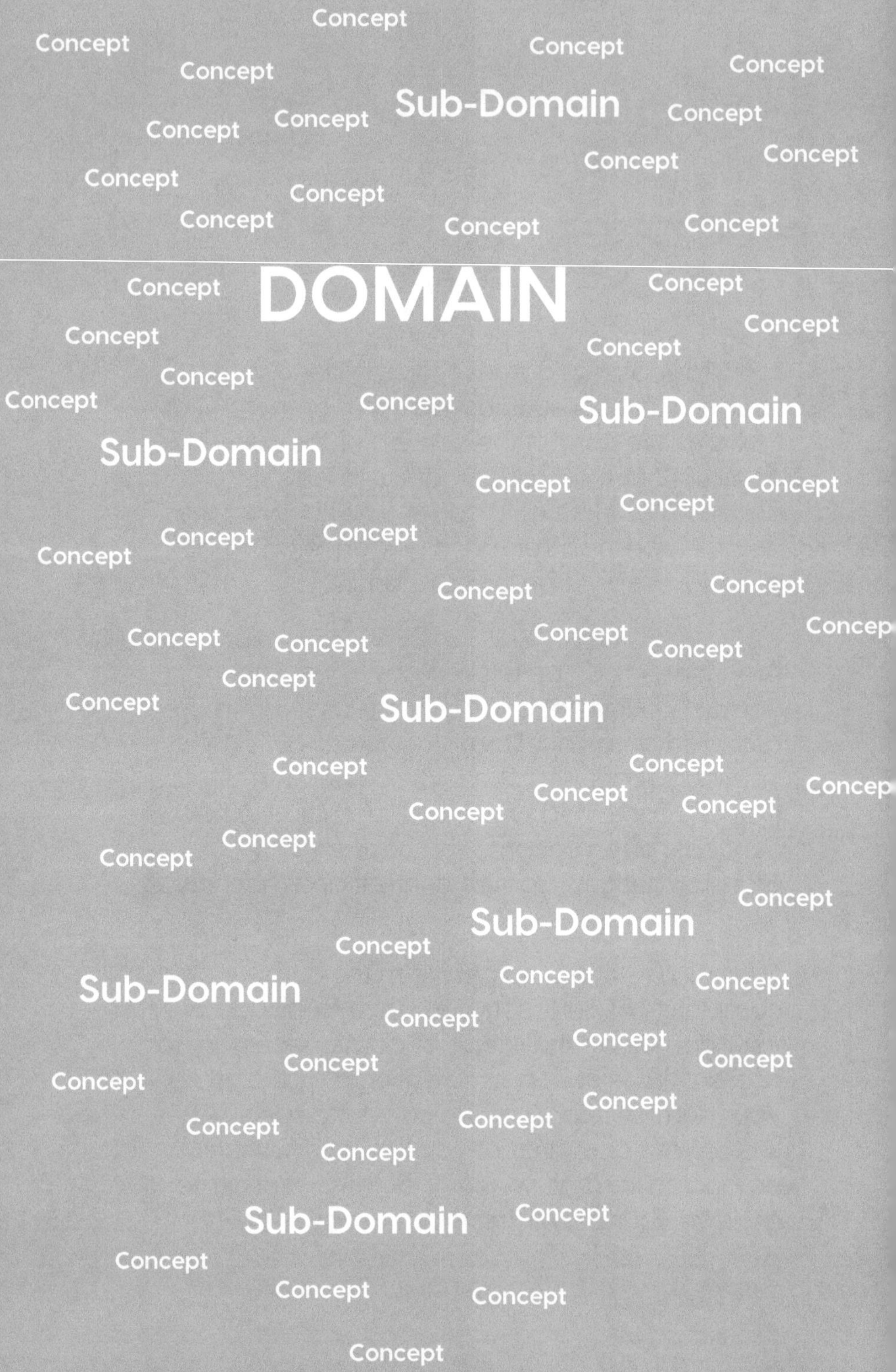
Concept
Concept
Concept
Concept
Concept
Sub-Domain
Concept
Concept
Concept
Concept
Concept
Concept
Concept
Concept
Concept
Concept
Concept
DOMAIN
Concept
Concept
Concept
Concept
Concept
Concept
Concept
Sub-Domain
Sub-Domain
Concept
Concept
Concept
Concept
Concept
Concept
Concept
Concept
Concep
Concept
Concept
Concept
Concept
Concept
Concept
Sub-Domain
Concept
Concept
Concep
Concept
Concept
Concept
Concept
Concept
Concept
Sub-Domain
Concept
Concept
Concept
Sub-Domain
Concept
Concept
Concept
Concept
Concept
Concept
Concept
Concept
Concept
Sub-Domain
Concept
Concept
Concept
Concept
Concept

The Need to Go Beyond Domain

The domain of your game is the subject matter your game covers. This is determined by your high-level purpose, player transformations, and barriers. Some examples of domains include physics, nutrition, civic engagement, language, fitness, etc. It's not uncommon to hear someone refer to the domain of a Transformational game as shorthand for what the game is – for example "a language game", or a "math game", etc. Of course, if you look closer at any domain, you will find that it can be broken down further into more specific sub-domains, for example, a *German* language game or a *geometry* game.

Your game will most likely not be able to thoroughly and exhaustively cover everything within your domain. It is also likely that your team members and other stakeholders have a varying understanding of what's in your domain and what matters within it.

E.g., You are working on a language game with player transformations related to learning Japanese and improving Japanese fluency. You might think that obviously your game will need to cover Japanese vocabulary. But what kind of vocabulary? Are there particular language interactions you are trying to support? Are you going to focus on listening, speaking, reading, writing, or all four? Will you cover specific topics? For example, will you include vocabulary on foods? What about baking? What about medicine? How much grammar will you include? Will you cover any aspects of Japanese culture? Japanese has formal and informal ways of speaking – will you cover both? What about including additional language learning strategies like teaching players how to look up words in a Japanese dictionary?

These are all concepts that could conceivably have a place in a game with a purpose to improve Japanese fluency. And, of course, there are many other possibilities.

You will need to identify the parts of your domain that you believe you need to impart to your players to support their transformation. The first step is to break your domain down into concepts. Once you have built a shared sense of what is within your domain, you can start to determine the most critical pieces to embody and incorporate into your game design.

Types of Concepts

"Concepts" is an abstract word and accordingly encompasses a wide variety of ideas from within a domain. In its most concrete forms, "concept" is often reduced to things like facts, definitions, or processes. As you explore your domain consider these, but also include a broader view of concepts. Here are some categories of concepts to prime your thinking:

For references on how games embody concepts, see Appendix M.

- **Factual:** data, definitions, people, places, things, and events
  E.g., The order and attributes of the eight planets in the solar system
- **Semiotic:** conventions such as categories, symbols, and terminology
  E.g., The symbols that represent the eight planets in the solar system
- **Procedural:** step-by-step, rules, techniques, and patterns
  E.g., How to calculate the distance of a planet using geometry
- **Explanations:** cause-and-effect, principles, and analysis
  E.g., The cause of the orbit speed of each planet in solar system
- **Narratives:** stories, themes, and anecdotes
  E.g., The story of the discovery of Uranus
- **Affects:** atmosphere, setting, relationships, emotions, and mindsets
  E.g., The historical tension of scientific discovery and religious entities
- **Practice:** experience, role-play, and firsthand memories
  E.g., Actual practice locating planets in the night sky

As with transformation types and barrier types, this list is not intended to be exhaustive or definitive. It is not important to label your domain concepts as a particular type or that they fit neatly into this list. The goal of this list is to help you and your team document the concepts that matter for your purposes by broadening your perception of what might count as a concept.

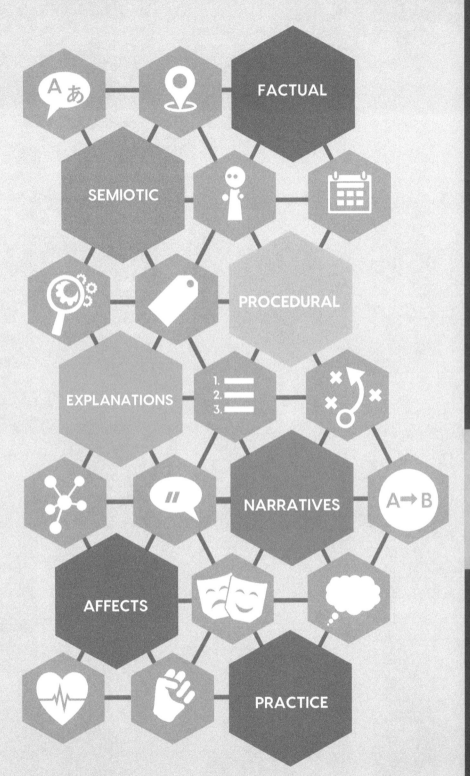

In vs Out
What are your boundaries?

Key vs Peripheral
What must remain on the main path?

In vs Out,
Key vs Peripheral

The primary benefit of establishing your domain concepts is determining what your game will include and exclude about your domain. Here are two ways to talk about this coverage:

Define boundaries between what's in and what's out.
Every concept that you want to convey to your players will need to be supported in some way by your game design and the game content you develop. Each will require some level of your time and attention. Look for areas of your domain that you can completely cut from your sphere of attention. Be sure to articulate with your team why that boundary exists.

E.g., You are working on a game with the domain of human biology. You decide that your game is intentionally not going to include any references to the body's lymphatic or nervous systems. This allows you to focus your resources on representing other aspects of human biology you wish to tackle.

Distinguish between what is key and what is peripheral.
Key concepts are what you believe players must engage with strongly in order to be effectively transformed in a way that transfers to the real world. Players aren't going to remember every fact, idea, or experience in your game. Your central concepts should be those things that you want to stick with every player. Thus these should become inspiration for game systems and content that will be on the main path of your game – something that players engage with repeatedly with significant impact on their play experience.

In contrast, peripheral concepts are those that you feel do support your player transformations but may not be critical. These may then translate into side content in your game that not every player will engage with or that players only engage with briefly. When it comes time to cut the scope of your game systems or your content, be wary of cutting what is key. Instead, look to your peripheral concepts to see what can be moved from "peripheral but in" to simply "out."

E.g., You are working on a game with the domain of the works of Shakespeare. You decide to include some domain concepts on four of his most famous plays, but you choose the plot of one, Hamlet, as your key content. This means the most emphasized content in your game will be about Hamlet. As development continues, you find you need to trim your scope. You keep the Hamlet content and cut one of the other three plays completely. You decide to frame the content related to the two remaining peripheral plays as comparisons and contrasts to Hamlet, so that the focus always stays on your chosen key concepts.

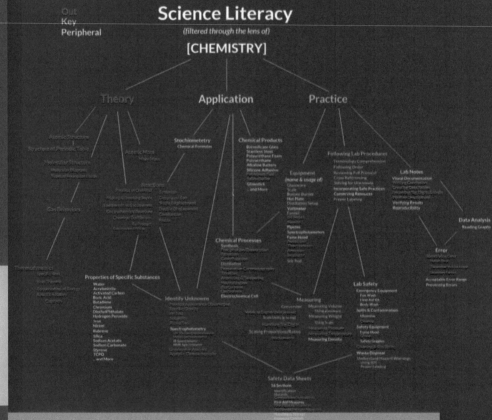

An example early concept map for a science literacy game based on the domain of chemistry.

Mapping Out Your Domain Concepts

To build your understanding of the concepts your domain encompasses, leverage sources that already attempt to break down your domain. For most domains, there will be multiple sources who have created variations of concept lists. It can take a little time to sift through various sources, but it can also be a huge boost if you find a source that provides a conceptual breakdown that feels good for your purposes. Some sources to explore are:

More about experts in the next chapter, **Expert Resources**.

- **Experts** who have a deep background in your domain
- **Books about your domain,** particularly textbooks or books designed to give an overview of the domain to non-experts
- **Educational standards** such as Common Core or Next Generation Science Standards
- **Course Syllabi** which may offer a breakdown of topics covered during the course
- **Assessments and Certifications** which often provide public listings of the concepts they cover

For more on educational standards, see Appendix N.

Consider making a visual map of your domain concepts.
You can document your domain concepts in a text-only format by generating a list, however, it can also be useful to take a visual approach that allows you to indicate relationships between sub-domains and concepts. A useful tool for doing so is to create a **concept map**. Concept maps are an approach to breaking down a top-level concept into a visual tree of subtopics. Their key features are:

Concept maps were developed by Joseph Novak. For references working with concept maps, see Appendix O.

- A **hierarchal structure** where the broadest part of the concept is at the top of the tree and the sub-topics tend to get more specific as depth increases.
- Sub-topics are connected through **cross-links** that indicate a relationship between the them.

As you build out your map of concepts, you may struggle with how granular to go. There is no perfect answer to this question. Go as granular as you need to be able to clarify your game's coverage of concepts and a general sense of the content you'll need to create to support them. You may find that you need to go more granular as development progresses.

The Domain of Water Bears

Water Bears[1] is a mobile puzzle game developed by Schell Games, designed to help teach systems thinking in middle school classrooms. In order to be financially viable for the studio, it also needed to stand on its own as an engaging game in the App Store. Oh, and it also needed to be built with a small team on a tight timeline. What else is new?

Water Bears uses puzzle mechanics to create hands-on demonstrations of systems thinking concepts.

Luckily, a prototype of the core mechanic had already been built. It was even created with systems thinking in mind and in collaboration with a subject-matter expert, but by a different team. Our new team needed to get up to speed quickly, so we connected with the subject-matter expert ourselves and tried to absorb all the written material we could find. The more we learned, the more we realized just how hard it was going to be to teach such a complex and amorphous subject. We knew we needed a way to map systems thinking concepts onto our game, but we were having trouble even understanding what all of the parts of the domain were.

Among the various reference materials we had collected was a book[2] our subject-matter expert was working on. Tucked into the back of this book, all the way in Appendix D, were a set of "Systems Thinking Concept Cards", meant to be cut out and referenced as bite-sized explanations of various components of systems thinking. These cards were the key to wrapping our own heads around systems thinking, and they were the perfect landscape on which to draw our domain concept map.

As we started to break down our domain and figure out how it fit with our game, we realized we had another problem. The puzzles and mechanics in *Water Bears* do a great job of embodying systems thinking concepts, but they don't teach those concepts at all. We knew that just pasting some explanations next to each puzzle wasn't going to be effective (players don't read!), but we didn't have the scope to do a much deeper integration, and we weren't sure it would be effective if we did.

[1-2] Find references for this developer story in Appendix P.

At this point we stumbled on a key insight: Our game *shouldn't* be trying to "teach" systems thinking! Teachers can do that so much better! Instead, our game can be a tool for teachers to use, giving students hands-on experience with systems thinking concepts, which is a real need for a subject that deals with the large, abstract systems of the modern world. Our domain concepts map ended up being broad but shallow, connecting many different systems thinking concepts to puzzles in the game, but not diving into any deep explanations. We provided lesson plans and level guides to teachers, though, to help guide them with relating the game to the subject matter.

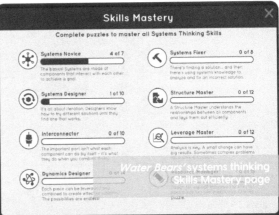

Water Bears' systems thinking Skills Mastery page

There was one big roadblock left. The way game mechanics are introduced in a puzzle game can be critical to player on-boarding and a sense of progression, so the order of our levels and level packs had to be carefully constructed to meet those needs. Our domain concept map didn't match that structure directly, though. To address this, we ended up creating a skills mastery system that worked in parallel to the natural progression of the game. Each time a player completes a puzzle, they level up in the skills (i.e., systems thinking concepts) related to that puzzle. Players can see their progress on each skill on a dedicated skills-mastery page that includes a very brief descriptions for each concept, derived directly from the Systems Thinking Concept Cards we had discovered in Appendix D.

By mapping out the landscape of systems-thinking domain concepts and putting it just under the surface of an otherwise delightful puzzle game, we tried to give both students and teachers exactly what they need to unlock understanding of a difficult subject.

Jason Pratt
Project Director, Water Bears

**Shared Understanding
Of Domain**

**Preview of
Content Scope**

**Coverage
Expectations**

Why Mapping Domain Concepts Matters

Creating a map of your domain concepts for your game provides several key benefits for your team.

It facilitates a shared domain understanding with your team and stakeholders. You may have noticed that one of the themes of the Framework is the idea that having a shared vocabulary is vital to collaborative problem solving. There are many ways to divvy up a particular domain into sub-domains and concepts. Creating your concept map is not about establishing the one true breakdown. It is about establishing a shared breakdown with your team – one that allows you to discuss your domain with the level of granularity needed to talk about what is essential.

It gives you a preview of the scope of domain concepts you will need to embody in your game. Even before you list out every individual fact or process step that must be included in the game, your concept map will help you gut check the quantity and complexity of the content you plan to fit into your game and your gameplay experience. This is essentially answering the question of how much game you need to build, with how many different systems and how much unique content you must design. You should be able to look at your concept map and believe that you can convey the key concepts well in the game you are designing given the resources you have available to you.

It sets expectations about what your game will cover. Your concept map outlines visibly what should be in the game, what should be core to the game vs what is ancillary, and should include documentation on your reasoning for these decisions. This helps you respond to feedback from both internal stakeholders during development, as well as external users or critics upon release. You will almost certainly get feedback asking for something to be added to or removed from your game. Your concept map allows you to reflect on this feedback, to say it was an intentional decision (hopefully) and to explain why.

Questions to Ask:

❑ Looking at what is marked as in, can you handle the scope it implies for content and game systems?

❑ Is there anything you are including that might be too difficult for your team, or risk causing your team a major distraction?

❑ Is there anything you could cut based on your understanding of your audience's initial state?

❑ Looking at what is marked as out, is there anything that important stakeholders will strongly miss? Can you justify its exclusion?

❑ Are there any points of tension across boundaries of what's in and out?

❑ Looking at what you've decided is key, if players only took these concepts from your game, would you consider that a success?

❑ Looking at what you've decided is peripheral, do you believe each item adds tangible value? Could you ship if you had to cut all of them completely?

❑ Consider each of your player transformations and barriers – have you included the domain concepts necessary to address each one? Do you need to revisit these pieces of your framework?

❑ Does anything on your map surprise you?

Vetting Your Concept Decisions

Once you have a sense of the landscape of your domain, you can start making decisions about boundaries and main path.

If you have created a visual map of your domain, you can use dotted lines to show boundaries and color variation to differentiate key verses peripheral concepts.

For each decision, articulate your whys: Why is something in or out? Why is something key or peripheral? To do so, consider the following tools:

- **Cross-reference with audience's initial state:** If you expect most of your players to come to your game with certain prior knowledge, perhaps you can leave these concepts out of your game, or treat them only as peripheral. On the other hand, it may be that you find some portions of your audience are missing some prerequisite concepts that aren't exactly part of your domain but are necessary for successful interactions with your domain concepts.

- **Leverage your player transformations and barriers:** Go through your list of player transformations and discuss what specific concepts of your domain need to be absorbed by your players to achieve that transformation. Do the same with your barriers. Each of these may give you slightly different insights into what is essential and why.

- **Look for connections that cross your boundaries:** What is out that might cause tension because it's tightly connected to something that's in? Does it belong in? Or is there something that is currently in that perhaps should be out?

- **Avoid "cans of worms":** Some topics in a domain are particularly hard to take on. They might be controversial. They might be very complex. They might highlight other domain content you are not including. Take on these difficult topics with eyes open... or, drop them completely.

- **Consider stakeholder audience expectations:** There may be aspects of your domain that you should include, not because you feel it is essential, but because you know that some stakeholders will be put off if they don't see it.

Consider the Impact to Scope

How do your domain concepts give you a sense of your game's scope? The answer is that, while it can't do so with complete certainty, it can give you a quick back-of-the-envelope sense of how big your game experience will need to be.

For each concept you are considering as "in," evaluate its scale and potential development burden. In other words, how much content will your team need to develop to successfully embody that concept? What are your initial thoughts on how to embody that concept through game content? Do you have the resources available to create that content?

Let's take a very simple example as an illustration:

Your central domain concepts include a set of about 100 new vocabulary words you'd like players to be able to recall after playing your game. For each of these 100 words, you'll need at least one game moment where players will engage with this content in a way that is memorable enough to persist and transfer beyond the game. If you're contemplating a game design with levels, think about how many words it might make sense to introduce in a single level – this gives you a sense of how many levels you might need. Also consider simply the rate of words over time. If you introduce just 1 word a minute, your game will be at least an hour and half long.

These are just quick calculations, of course, but they can help you understand if your domain concept decisions are reasonable or too ambitious. And they can push you towards or away from certain approaches based on the resources you have for development. You could design a game where each of these 100 interactions is a hand-crafted, unique branching character dialogue. Or you could design a game where the words are presented dynamically inside a re-playable game structure such as a puzzle. For each of these approaches, there are trade-offs in terms of the quality of the player's interaction with the domain concepts and the development costs required.

Question #6

Who knows what you don't know you don't know?

Expert
Resources

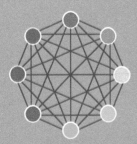

Who knows what
you don't know
you don't know?

It's unlikely that you and everyone on your team has a deep, professional background in your game's domain, how to represent it, and how to teach it. To help you navigate your game's domain, you should establish your **Expert Resources**. One of the most helpful form of expert resource you can involve in your process is a live person who takes on the role of your Subject-Matter Expert (SME).

Finding an SME typically requires seeking connections in communities beyond the discipline of game development. It also requires developing strategies for embedding your SME into your process. Of course, there will be overhead in integrating an SME into your work, especially someone who may be unfamiliar with games or who comes from a very different discipline background. However, a good SME partnership will provide significant positive influences on your design and can be critical for transformational success.

Credibility

Expertise

References

Subject-Matter
Perspective

Product
Advocate

Interpret
Feedback

The Value
of Experts

You should have a subject-matter expert working with you in some way on your Transformational game.

You should bring a subject-matter expert into your process as early as possible.

Working with a subject-matter expert at the start of pre-production can help you more quickly and accurately establish your Transformational Framework.

SMEs serve multiple purposes:

- **Credibility:** An SME can signal to external audiences that your game has been vetted.
- **Expertise:** An SME can bring a deep understanding of the domain concepts, including relevant barriers.
- **Reference:** An SME can provide a rich knowledge of the literature and prior work you should review. They can point you quickly to quality subject-matter references you can leverage to inform your design.
- **Subject-Matter Perspective:** An SME can be strong voice on behalf of the subject-matter content and/or pedagogy represented in your game*.
- **Product Advocate:** An SME can provide support and promotion of your game to their own communities.
- **Interpretation:** An SME can provide a filter to interpret feedback from other experts & stakeholders, as well as results from testing.

Your SME does not have to be a person. You might also use reference materials as a way to get SME input into your project when you don't have access to a person.

*YOU should also champion these things but your attention will necessarily be split with the player experience around issues of gameplay and engagement.

Structuring the SME Role

Teams are often unsure of how they should be using SMEs – how often they should be talking to them, whether or not they need to be paid, and how much weight their feedback should have. There is no single answer, but here are four generalized patterns:

- **Consultant:** This is someone you bring in one time or on-demand as needed. You might meet with them in-person early in the design process to get an initial dump of information about the domain, or you might get their occasional input throughout development. In this role, your expert is typically providing input in direct response to questions you pose to them. Many experts are generous about sharing their expertise through informal consultation, even if you can't provide compensation.

- **Reviewer:** This is someone you are asking to look at your documents or game builds in detail and provide feedback on them based on their expertise. You might only ask them to do this once, or you might ask them to do so on an ongoing basis. They might not be compensated directly but they are often stakeholders with some kind of vested interest in your game's development.

- **Advisor:** This is someone with whom you have regularly scheduled interactions through development. In this role, experts often serve as a sounding board for key design decisions and milestones. This role is likely to be compensated.

- **Partner:** This is someone who is working closely with your team. They interact with the team regularly and are involved in ongoing discussions and decisions about the game's development. In this role, experts may be actually producing documents or even game content. Experts serving in this role are almost always compensated in some way for their work.

You may find you need to blend between these roles or transition your SME from role to role over the course of your project:

The Consultant
On-Demand Advice on Specific Questions

- Need-driven communication
- Infrequent or informal interactions
- Compensation might not be needed

The Reviewer
Feedback on Progress Milestones

- Responds to builds or documents
- Validates or challenges what you produce
- Might not be paid but might be a stakeholder

The Advisor
Regular Open-Ended Discussions

- Regularly scheduled interactions
- Sounding board for direction and subject-matter questions
- More likely to be compensated

The Partner
Part of the Team

- Close working relationship
- Formally or Informally part of the team
- Most likely paid (sometimes by your client)
- May produce some content

More Responsibility

- EXPERT RESOURCES -

 Leverage
Team's
Network

 Find the
Thought
Leaders

 Seek out
Communities
of Practice

 Reach Out
to Schools &
Universities

 Look to Other
Intervention
Programs

Channels for Finding an Expert

Okay, you're convinced you need a Subject-Matter Expert and you have some ideas about the role you'd like them to play with your team, but how should you go about finding one? Here are some channels you can use to seek and find your SME:

Take advantage of the team's network. A personal connection is a powerful way to recruit an SME. Ask your team and other stakeholders to reach out through their personal networks.

Reach out to thought leaders. Find out who the thought leaders are in your domain space by looking at authors of key publications, well-known speakers, or prominent, respected voices in social media channels. Highly visible thought leaders may be too busy to work with you directly, but they are often well-connected and might be able to point you to someone else.

Seek out the domain's community of practice. Where do people in your domain space engage with each other for professional development? Look for online communities and key conferences where you could share a solicitation for collaboration.

Reach out to local schools & universities. Teachers can make great SMEs because they have practice explaining their domain to others. And if your game is meant to be used by a student audience or is meant to be used in a classroom setting with teacher facilitation, then working with a teacher can give you useful insights into your Audience & Context. At the university level, you may find SMEs who are researchers focused on learning or teaching your subject matter, which can be a beneficial perspective.

Look at other initiatives. Look for other people who are also tackling your high-level purpose through other intervention programs. For example, if your game's purpose is to reduce smoking in teens, then consider working with individuals who run smoking cessation programs for teens in your community. These programs may already be connected to strong expert resources.

An Ideal SME

- Is available as needed
- Can be supported within project resources
- Can provide the range or depth of expertise needed
- Can be a bridge to non-experts
- On-board with game approach
- Can collaborate well

What
to Look For

Like any working relationship, you're looking for more in an SME than expertise. When considering a potential SME, take these additional factors into account:

- **What is their availability?** Do they have time to commit to your project at the level and frequency that you need? Be clear about the model of relationship you are looking for – Consultant, Reviewer, Advisor, or Partner – and the time commitment it would involve.

- **What are their needs?** What do they need to stay motivated in their involvement? Are they professionally motivated? Do they require compensation? Do they want any formal recognition of their role? Can they convince their organization or institution that collaborating with your team is a good idea?

- **Can they cover the breadth and depth you need?** Make sure your potential SME has the range or depth of expertise you need. Or that they can guide you to that depth or breadth through their familiarity and connections in the subject-matter space.

- **Can they bridge the gap between expert and non-expert?** It's really helpful if your SME has experience and skill at breaking down the subject matter with a level of clarity and simplicity that makes it accessible to non-experts. This will help your SME communicate with your team. And it will enable your SME to better advise you on how to effectively reach your player audience.

- **Are they open to (or better yet, excited by) a game approach?** Your SME doesn't need to be a gamer, but if you're looking for more than an one-time consultant, it helps if they are supportive of the idea of creating a game for your purpose.

- **Will they be good collaborators?** Transformational games inevitably involve compromise between the game experience and the subject matter. Beware of SMEs who consider everything in their subject matter to be sacred. They may struggle to accept accommodations to the subject-matter material due to the game medium, player experience, or available resources.
  In a similar vein, an SME who wants to contribute heavily to the game design but doesn't respect your expertise in this area (or their own limitations) can also lead to friction.

Some Common Mistakes With SMEs

These mistakes boil down to effectively one thing: Not using an SME to inform your pre-production and early design.

Mistake #1: Not having an SME. This can happen when your timeline is short or you don't have the funds. Or if you think you can just learn the material yourself. Generally speaking, this is a bad idea that at best leaves you focusing on the wrong things, and at worst leaves you just plain getting things wrong.

Mistake #2: Getting an SME too late. Your SME is most valuable as a foundational tool to inform your design early in your process, not just a rubber stamp at the end to validate what you've built. The outcome here can end up the same as not having an SME at all, except that you'll find out what you got wrong in time to do something about it, provided you have the resources and flexibility to make changes.

Mistake #3: Overlooking the need for multiple SMEs. You need an SME with expertise in your domain topic. However, you might also benefit from an SME who is familiar with the audience or context in which your game will be played, or someone with a background in learning science, instructional design, behavioral theory, or other disciplines that relate to teaching and changing people.

Mistake #4: Defaulting to the client as the SME. Sometimes on client-based Transformational games, the client has a background in the subject matter. This can be a great asset to a team but it also comes with risks. Clients serving as SMEs are, by definition, doing at least double duty in their role on a project. This can create confusing priorities for everyone, so take care in this scenario. Be sure to identify exactly who on the client side will be serving as the primary SME. Take the time to discuss the parameters of their role. Honestly consider what's needed in an SME for your game. You may find that your client isn't available enough for your SME needs, or that their expertise doesn't actually cover what you require. It can be awkward to suggest bringing in an additional SME when working with an expert client, but sometimes it is necessary.

Even if you can't find someone who can give an ongoing commitment, make every effort to at least get a 1-2 hour conversation with someone deeply knowledgeable on the relevant topic(s).

Remember, you don't know what you don't know.

Tips for Working With SMEs

- 1 -

Listen respectfully. Even if your SME has no official approval role on your team, you should treat their input seriously, listen respectfully, and work to build consensus with them on how the gameplay reflects the subject matter and supports the player transformation. If your SME feels like their advice falls on deaf ears, they are less likely to provide thoughtful information and feedback next time.

- 2 -

Share your design approach. Remember that it is likely your SME may be unfamiliar with games and that their primary role is to promote the subject-matter focus of the game. If you decide that you will not or cannot take their suggestions, make sure you spend the time to share with them your reasoning for your design choices in an accessible way so that they can understand your approach to the player experience and the realities of the resources available to your team. Not only can this help keep them engaged, it can give them better context for their future feedback.

- 3 -

Fewer design docs, more show & tell. If you want SME feedback on your game design approach, don't rely on sharing design documentation meant for the development team. This form of documentation is often not accessible for non-developers. Instead, use narrative-based scenarios paired with visuals to help make the connection between gameplay and the subject-matter material it is supposed to embody. If you have a working prototype, consider having your SME observe a playtest so that they can really see how players engage with the material through the game.

- 4 -

Do not rely on SMEs for game development questions. Your SME is not a game designer. They are not responsible for the quality of the player experience – You are. Don't expect them to be able to answer questions related to pacing, engagement, or gameplay. Don't expect them to value these things higher than the elements of the game that represent their expertise. Sometimes SMEs themselves may try to take on the role of a game designer. This can be especially tricky to navigate if your SME has a partner role or is your client. Respect each other's input in all areas, but also respect each other's unique areas of expertise and leverage them.

- 5 -

Remember that all domains have schools of thought. Biases and prioritization differences exist in nearly all domains. Politics also exists in places you might never expect. Keep this in mind as you talk with experts. Make an effort to understand the specific perspectives of your SMEs and other stakeholders. If you find multiple key stakeholders with divergent priorities and approaches, consider establishing the 'official' approach for your game. Document these decisions so your team and subject-matter partners can reference them through development.

- 6 -

Be sensitive to triggers when soliciting feedback. Terminology matters – your SME will care if you are using the vocabulary of their domain incorrectly. Factual accuracy matters – your SME will care if your content directly or indirectly says something that isn't true about their domain. Authenticity matters – your SME will care if you represent the culture of their domain incorrectly. If you're sharing a game build or documentation, be aware that these details can be a distraction for SMEs, even if you express that the content is temporary or in-progress.

DEV SPEAK

"So at the end of this sprint, we'll have a playable prototype with all the basic functionality of an endless runner. We'll be using a white boxed environment, mocked up in Unity. We'll share the GDD with you via g-drive."

Watch out for:
- Game dev jargon
- Game references
- Tech jargon

SME SPEAK

"Can we talk about how the theoretical framework for the relevant key mediators is informed by theories on self-efficacy and social norms related to chemistry? Also, I don't see how this explains the nuances of covalent bonding."

Watch out for:
- Academic jargon
- Subject-matter jargon

Engage in Cultural Exchange

Because Transformational games often involve collaborations between game developers and non-game developers, subject-matter experts and non-subject-matter experts, part of preparing to work on the Framework is taking some time to share knowledge across these discipline boundaries.

Before you really dig into working with your SME (or client!), make sure you take some time to do a cultural exchange between your development team and these non-game industry stakeholders. The purpose of this exchange is for each side to share enough information about their respective disciplines to enable everyone to talk comfortably to one another without feeling lost in jargon.

It's important for your dev team to gain at least a high-level understanding of the subject matter.

- What are the big concepts that this domain is built on? What domain-specific vocabulary is common when discussing the subject matter?

- Who or what are the subject-matter expert resources that represent the core information about the subject matter and reflect your SME's approach to the topic?

- What are the most critical reference materials your team should actually acquire and consume?

Solicit this information from your SMEs and engage with it seriously. It's not necessary to make it your goal to become an expert yourself in the domain space, but you do need to be able to feel comfortable around the language.

Your client or SME may be new to game development, so share some grounding information about the game dev process.

- Share the Game Development Primer in this book, being sure to call out what does (or doesn't) apply to your particular process

- Clarify what feedback process will be used to incorporate comments from the client.

- For experts that will be involved as an advisor or a partner, it can be especially helpful to suggest some games for them to play on their own that might serve as good references for your project.

Night Shift's SME

❝ From the day the Night Shift[1] project presented itself at Schell Games as a game to change how ER doctors think and make decisions, we realized that close collaboration with a subject-matter expert would be essential to its success. We knew nothing about making games for doctors, let alone one trying to simulate an actual work shift at an Emergency Room.

Fortunately, we got very lucky. Dr. Deepika Mohan was our client, and the recipient of the grant that allowed Night Shift to be created. Most importantly though, she was dedicated to be part of our team and support the development in any way she could. The fact that Dr. Mohan lived and worked in the same city as our team meant we could meet face-to-face as often as felt necessary, and it made all the difference.

The first step to our successful partnership was to establish a common language. We set up a meeting in which we used a draft copy of this very book to present to her how we, as game developers, think about bringing about change in the player. From her end, we learned a bit about the behavioral science theory behind her research, and basics of triaging trauma patients.

Another outcome of this exercise was a building of trust. We understood Dr. Mohan's vision, and she gained confidence in our development process. Even though it was impossible for us to "catch up" on med school, we learned enough to understand how content created by our SME can fit into a point-and-click mystery adventure that aims to emotionally engage non-gamers, some of whom went as far as telling us they're "morally opposed to games" in a survey we conducted.

Night Shift asks players to take on the role of a small-town doctor in a narrative-driven point-and-click adventure game.

HOPEWELL COMMUNITY HOSPITAL
RECEPTION

[1-2] Find references for this developer story in Appendix Q.

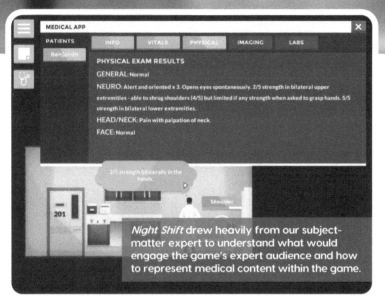

Night Shift drew heavily from our subject-matter expert to understand what would engage the game's expert audience and how to represent medical content within the game.

The other important facet of this dev-SME relationship was our focus on playtesting. Even with all the knowledge sharing, we realized that the real test will be to put our game prototype in front of actual medical staff, watch them play, and listen to what they have to say about it. It became quickly and vividly apparent that we had a LOT to learn about our target audience. Again, Dr. Mohan found ways to greatly help on this quest. She was able to consistently provide us with time, space, and volunteers to do this with, and went as far as creating a survey filled with Likert scale questions akin to those given to pilot audiences of TV shows to measure playtesters' engagement. We didn't like it. Our design minds reeled at the thought of judging a game like you would a TV show, but we trusted our SME and went along with it. The data we gathered ended up not only helping us to identify that engagement with our story was a problem, but also gave us a solid metric for gauging improvement when we took steps to remedy this.

This project concluded successfully, and was tested in a trial that indicated that doctors who played *Night Shift* showed significant improvement in trauma patient triage performance when compared to those given reading materials[2]. We continue to work with Dr. Mohan on follow-up projects, and benefit from her expertise.

Research reported in this publication was supported by the National Library of Medicine of the National Institutes of Health under award number DP2 LMO12339.c

Michal Ksiazkiewicz
Project Director, Night Shift

 Books

 Papers

 Videos

 Websites

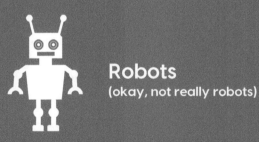 Robots
(okay, not really robots)

The Benefit of Non-Human Resources

In addition to seeking out an individual as an SME, it is a good idea to select a small body of vetted, relevant media resources that cover your subject matter. Create a media list of books, websites, and/or videos. Encourage your team to consume the items on the list. These media expert resources are helpful because they are pre-curated media about your domain. This means that someone else spent time and effort collecting a finite list of concepts, examples, best practices, etc. about your domain and presenting it in a coherent, linear manner. These sources are available at all times for your entire team. You can use them to help catch up new team members, or as reference when your SME is not available. Leveraging them as reference will make it easier to communicate with your SME.

Again, don't neglect the multiple aspects of your domain and audience. For example, if you are working on a game to change investment behavior in middle-class adults, your list of expert resources might include a book on investment, some research papers on middle-class investment behavior, and an investment documentary.

Some of these resources may overlap with your **Prior Works**, covered in the next chapter.

A human SME can be a great boon to a project but sometimes it's hard to find someone who can integrate with your team in the role you need or want. If this is the case, put special emphasis on identifying your short list of expert media resources for your team. Seek expert recommendations for the best materials. A book or paper recommendation might be something an expert can pass along to you quickly, even if they are not available to take on a larger role with your project.

Question
#7

What can you learn from what others have done?

Prior Works

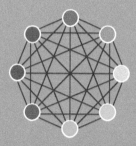

What can you
learn from what
others have done?

It is valuable to your team, and to the advancement of Transformational games on the whole, to learn from the **Prior Works** of others. Doing so allows your team to build up from prior successes, adapt from prior failures, and to benefit from prior exploration and thinking into your design space.

Keep in mind that your design space includes both the realm of games and the realm of transformation. In that vein, "prior work" here is used as a broad term to include other interventions (games or otherwise) as well as research that connects to other pieces of your transformational framework such as your purpose, transformations, audience, barriers, etc.

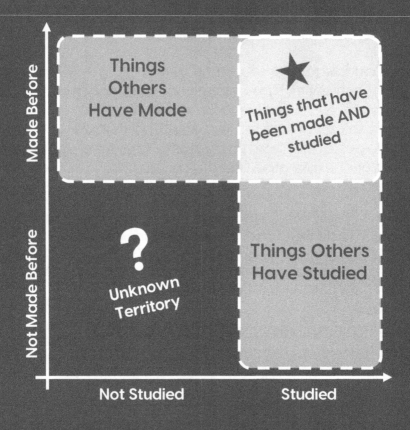

What are
Prior Works?

Prior works are references you can use to inform your game's transformational approach.
Entertainment game development often draws inspiration from prior works. For example, you might use images from a movie to express the look and feel you're aiming for in your game. Or you might refer to a particular set of mechanics in a published game to illustrate how your own game's system will work. These kinds of gameplay and aesthetic references are also useful in Transformational game development. But for the purposes of your transformational framework, prior work here is intended to be references for your game's transformational aspects, giving a preview into two important questions:

- What could your implementation look like?
- Is your implementation likely to work?

Some prior works are things others have made.
The most obvious prior work is something that looks very much like what you're trying to do – a game with a similar transformational purpose. However, games are not the only medium used to try to transform people. Prior works can also include films, books, courses, and more. These works help illustrate what implementation approaches are possible.

Some prior works are things others have studied.
Another category of prior work for Transformational games is what others have researched about the space of your transformational problem. This could include research on things others have made, but also broader research on your problem space itself – barriers, transformations, the domain, the audience, etc. These works help reveal things that are known about your transformational problem space, and they give insight into which implementation approaches might be more or less effective.

Prior works illuminate your transformational problem space by looking at what others before you have built or learned in that space.

Ready-Made Prototypes

Efficacy Indicators

Vetted Insights

The Value
of Prior Works

If you leverage prior works well, they represent some measure of work that you no longer have to do yourself.

Prior works can serve as ready-made prototypes.

Think of prior works (especially those where someone else built a working, testable thing) as something you can engage with as you might your own prototyping process. Prototypes are effectively implementation experiments – *what if it worked like this*? Take this mindset when examining prior works. Look at what they did, what worked, what didn't, what conclusions others drew about the work, and use this to inform your own steps forward. Remember, prior works do not have to be games and they can be used to inform more than the game design approach. For example, you can look at what data a prior work collected as insight into what data you might want to collect about your game and its impact.

Prior works can offer indicators for the potential effectiveness of a particular approach.
A major question for Transformational games is: Will they work? Looking at works built by others will allow you to see reaction to their impact – is there any evidence it works or any conclusions as to why or why not? Likewise, looking at research work allows you to benefit from the conclusions that others have already drawn from running experiments in your domain space. For example, research might show that introducing domain concepts in a certain particular order leads to stronger comprehension.

Prior works can offer vetted insights into your transformational problem space.
The Transformational Framework process is itself a kind of map of your design problem space. It is documentation of your team's understanding of this space: who the audience is, what the barriers are, how players must be transformed, what matters in the domain concepts, etc. Prior works represent someone else's exploration around some of these same questions. That is why previous chapters have referenced research and expert resources as methods of exploring pieces of the Framework. You have limited time to build your understanding of your problem space. You will be judged by others who are already very familiar to the space. Prior works help you quickly understand what others already know and leverage thinking that has been vetted by a larger community of stakeholders. If you're stuck understanding your problem or what approach to take, prior works can help.

Types of Prior Work

Let's further break down the landscape of prior works to get a fuller view of the spectrum it encompasses.

Related Interventions: Things Others Have Made

"Intervention" is a term that is used in some circles to talk about specific programs designed to change people. A related intervention is a product or experience that in some ways tackles the same purpose, player transformations, domain, or audience as your game. As the field of Transformational games grows, increasingly there may be an existing game intervention you can reference. But remember that when it comes to your high-level purpose, a game represents only one strategy. Consider interventions in other mediums, for example:

- A **class** experience with a teacher and peer group
- Other media such as **films**, **books**, or **audio**
- A **self-paced program** with materials that individuals progress through on their own
- An **entertainment game** adapted as an intervention

Supporting Research: Things Others Have Studied

Research refers to published theory based on rigorous experiments and analysis, conducted by trained researchers and vetted through a process which includes peer review.

Research is undertaken for four basic reasons:

- **Description:** Collect data on a phenomenon, often with the goal of being able to articulate generalities
  E.g., Research to measure the number of unique words that 14-year-olds use in their daily online discourse
- **Prediction:** Attempt to predict the results of one phenomenon from the observations of another
  E.g., Research that seeks to predict the long-term academic success of students based on their pre-K attendance
- **Control:** Attempt to change one phenomenon through the manipulation of another
  E.g., Research to test if exposure to a particular Transformational game results in the intended behavior change
- **Explanation:** Attempt to definitively establish the cause(s) of a phenomenon through the use of rigorous controls
  E.g., Research into the efficacy of a particular medicine through a trial that includes comparison to a placebo

Relevant supporting research can include general research into your domain or research on related interventions.

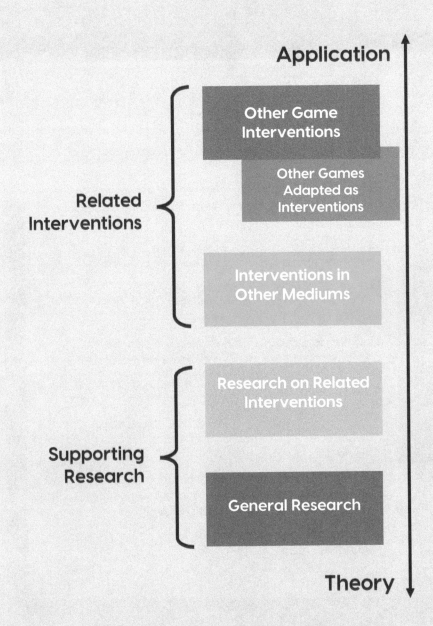

Questions to Ask:

- ❑ What are the structures and features of the intervention?

- ❑ What insights can you glean about the design decisions for the intervention and what informed these decisions?

- ❑ What domain content is embedded in the intervention and how is this content presented?

- ❑ How long, how often, and under what circumstances does the intervention's audience interact with the intervention?

- ❑ What assumptions does it seem the intervention makes about the audience? Are they accurate?

- ❑ What efficacy claims does the intervention make and how does it demonstrate its efficacy, if at all?

- ❑ If the intervention assesses impact on players, what data does it use to do so and how is this data collected and presented?

- ❑ What critiques, positive or negative, have been made of the intervention? (Include reviews by players AND non-player stakeholders)

- ❑ How does the medium of the intervention influence what you can take away for your game?

Using Related Interventions

Consult with your expert resources and stakeholder audiences to identify interventions that are worth examining. Look for organizations whose purpose aligns to your own and see what interventions they support or recommend.

Here are several techniques you can use to leverage related interventions, games or otherwise, as prior works:

- **Direct Review:** Personally play, participate, observe, or otherwise directly experience the intervention.
- **Playtest:** Run a playtest with your audience using the intervention and see for yourself how it works. This very practical technique is often overlooked by teams, who focus only on getting something of their own up for playtesting.
- **Post-Mortems:** Sometimes projects will publish reflective insight into their design rationale, success, and failures. These post-mortem reports might even include that project's own supporting research, or other materials similar to the pieces of the Transformational Framework, which you can examine for relevance to your own work.
- **3rd Party Review:** It's possible a related intervention has been studied and you can use this research to glean takeaways for your team. Even if a prior work has not been formally studied, you may be able to find some informal or anecdotal insight into its approach and efficacy, such as reviews or personal stories from experts and stakeholders. If you can't find existing quality reviews, you might ask someone with expertise related to your domain and audience to undertake a review on your behalf.

  For some example reviews of related interventions, see Appendix R.

- **Interview or Consult:** You can also contact the developers or researchers directly to ask them questions about how their interventions or playtests went, the lessons they learned, or their thoughts on future work that might build on what they did.

You are not looking at related interventions primarily to mimic their implementation. You are seeking to understand the decisions and strategies employed by someone else tackling your purpose, in order to inform your own approach.

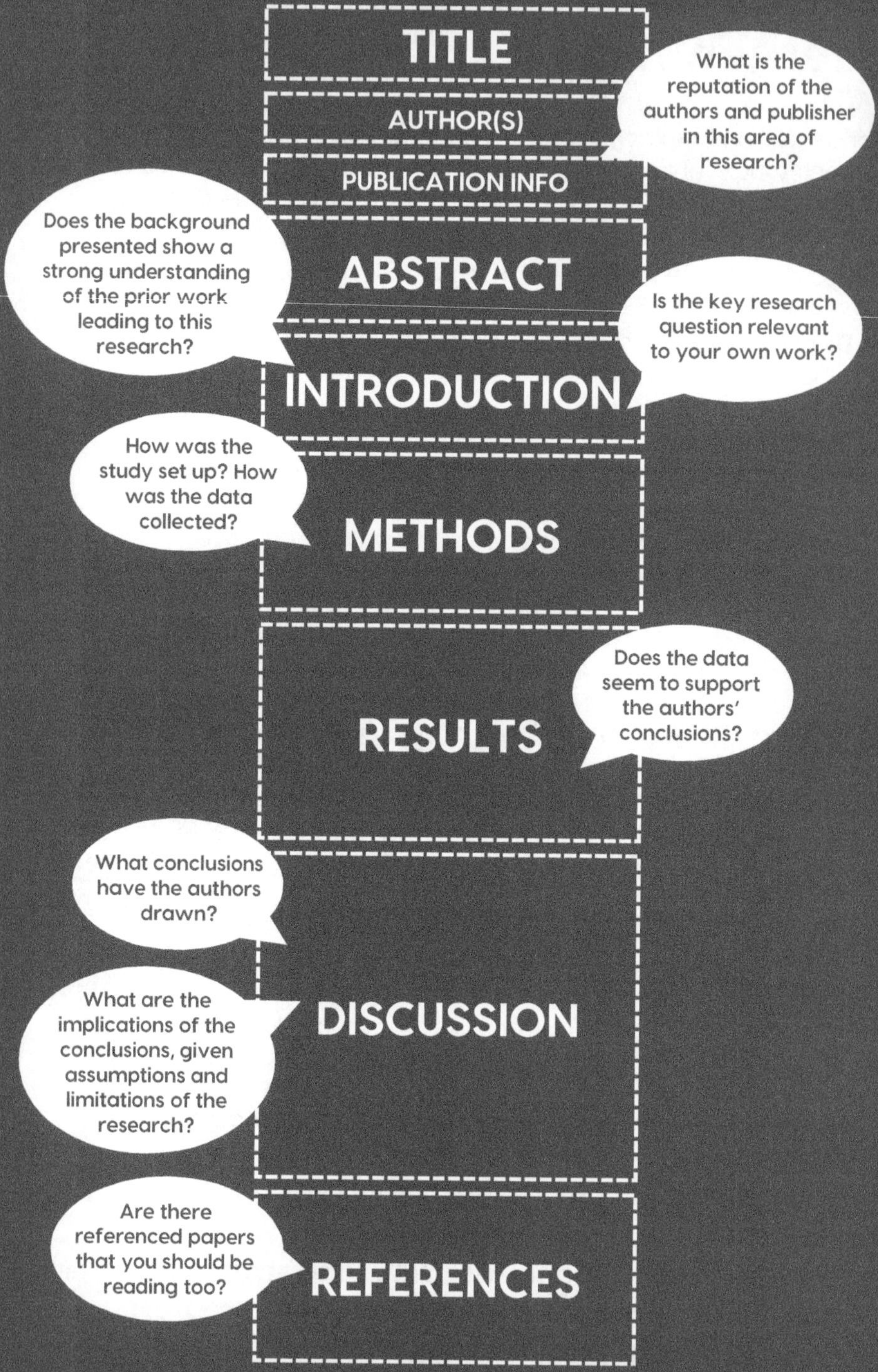
TITLE
What is the reputation of the authors and publisher in this area of research?
AUTHOR(S)
PUBLICATION INFO
Does the background presented show a strong understanding of the prior work leading to this research?
ABSTRACT
Is the key research question relevant to your own work?
INTRODUCTION
How was the study set up? How was the data collected?
METHODS
Does the data seem to support the authors' conclusions?
RESULTS
What conclusions have the authors drawn?
What are the implications of the conclusions, given assumptions and limitations of the research?
DISCUSSION
Are there referenced papers that you should be reading too?
REFERENCES

What's in a Research Paper?

Most research papers follow the same general format.
Understanding this format will help you quickly parse through papers to find ones relevant to you:

For more on reading research papers, see Appendix S.

- **Authors:** Most papers will have more than one author. *Often the first author is the project lead or largest contributor. In some cases, the last author is the senior researcher who heads the lab where the research was done.*
- **Publication Information:** Year published and publisher. *Online publications may also include a citation count, showing how many other papers have cited this paper.*
- **Abstract:** A summary of the research question and results. *Most online access portals for papers will allow you to read a paper's abstract even if the full paper is behind a paywall. However, don't base your work on the abstract alone. If the title and abstract seem promising, get a copy of the full paper to make sure you understand the full picture of the research.*
- **Introduction:** Background information on the research. *This should include important prior works and the key research question motivating the research work represented by the paper.*
- **Methods:** Details on how the research was conducted. *This will include information like how participants were recruited or specific questions asked.*
- **Results:** The actual data from the research.
- **Discussion:** Interpretation of the results. *The authors' conclusions based on the data collected. This may posit larger implications and suggest directions for future research.*
- **References:** Citations for works referenced by the paper.

Look for indicators of the study's overall quality.
Just because something is presented in a research paper format does not mean it meets the standards of quality research. Watch out for:

- **Conflict of interest:** Who funded the research? Are there competing interests on the part of the funders, authors, or publisher? The existence of a conflict doesn't automatically discredit a study but it indicates the need for extra scrutiny.
- **Irreputable publisher:** Some for-profit journals engage in pay-to-publish practices with questionable vetting of papers.
- **Specious Conclusions:** The paper should clearly connect the actual data collected to the conclusions reached, making clear any assumptions and limitations. Check on the sample size used in the study and look for indications that the results have been replicated.

Lessons Learned in Research

Using unreliable sources to advise decisions can have real consequences! During one of my graduate programs, we ran a preschool practicum program in which we based our classroom procedures on evidence-based practice. Parents would ask us why their child acted differently at school than at home, and it usually came down to the different strategies used across settings. For example, one parent reported giving a 5-year-old child a 5-minute time-out every time he threw a tantrum because they read about that strategy on a parenting website. Unfortunately, the child was throwing tantrums to get out of doing things that he didn't want to do. Not only did the time-out not work, but it was actually making the tantrums worse! Digging into additional resources surrounding that time-out recommendation would've saved the parents and child a lot of unnecessary frustration.

> "Evidence-based practice" describes interventions that are supported by solid data.

Having low-effort access to research online can be both a blessing and a curse, so it's essential to question the trustworthiness of sources and information. A good source is reputable, peer-reviewed, and holds quality of methods, results, and conclusions in the highest regard. Examining the connection between the data collected and the conclusions drawn is essential. Headlines and titles can be attention-grabbing, but it's important to check the original source for accuracy. The goal is to find and use evidence-based practice to inform decisions. "Evidence-based practice" describes the process of selecting interventions that are supported by solid data. This can be difficult because it requires high-quality studies that take time to plan, conduct, and disseminate. It's worth the effort, though, because it increases the likelihood of achieving a desired outcome because it draws on scientific knowledge rather than pseudoscience and ineffective (or potentially harmful) strategies.

At Schell Games, when we're deciding how we want our game experience to transform the player, we aim to use evidence-based practice to inspire game mechanics. It's not a silver bullet that guarantees success, but it is a strategy that

1-5 Find references for this developer story in Appendix T.

gives us the highest likelihood of it. We look for good sources, and evaluating them typically requires a bit of digging. Some "journals" might look legitimate, but their goal may be to make money rather than disseminate good data. These predatory journal practices can lead to false or faux findings that are published quickly in a highly accessible way (including even fake papers inspired by well-known sci-fi movies[1].)

> **At Schell Games, when we're deciding how we want our game experience to transform the player, we aim to use evidence-based practice to inspire game mechanics.**

Unfortunately, even reputable, peer-reviewed sources can be fallible. My dissertation work focused on improving children's dietary decisions[2]. A research group that came up in my literature review, the Cornell Food and Brand lab, was well-known for simple dietary interventions (e.g., using smaller plates[3], making unhealthy choices harder to reach[4], etc.) with big results, earning accolades and being published in highly regarded journals. More recently though, the lab and its director have come under fire for using very questionable methods to obtain results that would garner positive media coverage[5]. Fortunately, my work was not based on theirs and my studies and conclusions were unaffected, but what if it had been? Or, what if our studio had incorporated one of these ill-fated interventions into a transformational game? Not only would the transformation likely not be achieved, but the results could be potentially harmful to the player.

Whether new data and conclusions arise or poorly conducted studies fall away, it's important to remain in touch with the research you use so that you can respond if something like this happens. This challenge of balancing rigor, practicality, and potential curveballs shouldn't be underestimated; it can be difficult! Healthy doses of skepticism and flexibility about sources, data, conclusions, and the ever-changing nature of scientific research will go a long way.

Brooke Morrill, PhD
Director of Education
Schell Games

SMEs

Conferences

Lit
Reviews

SEARCH

Online
Databases

Check
Citations

Follow
Select Work

Gathering Research

Finding your supporting research can be a struggle, especially when using broad search tools like Google. Here are some more targeted approaches you can use:

- **Your subject-matter expert:** Start here. Your SME may be able to point you towards key research they are already familiar with that intersects with their expertise. This is a great way to jumpstart your search.
- **Consider conferences:** Many research communities hold conferences. Consider attending a conference to see what research is prominent in the community. These conferences often publish conference proceedings, which is a written record of the presented research. You might also look at who keynotes at conferences. These individuals may be thought leaders who have published important research.
- **Look for literature reviews:** These are secondary sources that review, aggregate and draw conclusions or patterns from research articles. This might be an academic book or sometimes might even be in the form of popular non-fiction.
- **Search online databases:** There are a number of research publication databases online. Often these online databases may share parts of an abstract or conclusions of papers for free, but may charge to see the full text. If you have access to a university through a subject-matter expert or another key stakeholder, their institution may have a subscription to one or more of these databases. Alternatively, sometimes authors will share their papers on their own professional websites or, if you email and ask nicely, they may be willing to send you the full text for free.

For some example online sources of research, see Appendix U.

- **Check citations:** Once you have at least one paper or book reference, follow its citations to find additional research. Most papers include an introduction that summarizes the relevant prior literature about their topic, and all academic papers will include citations at the end. Use these to find additional works.
- **Follow a particular expert's line of research:** If you find out about a particular thought leader in the field, check out their online CV or publication history. Look at both what other research they reference and the history of their own research. You can also reach out to invite them to participate in your work as an SME.

SME's Recommendation

Long-Standing Research

Recent Research

Actionable Application

Pick a Perspective

Filtering
Supporting Research

It's not realistic to hold up all related research as critical prior works to influence your design. You will need to pick a few sources that you will particularly rely on. Additionally, the validity of research may change over time. Sometimes past studies are invalidated after their results fail to be found reproducible. Sometimes a more nuanced understanding comes into acceptance over time. Filter your research influences, looking for a handful that provide a mix of these attributes:

- **Your SME's recommendation:** Find out what research is most important to your SME. Consider this research for your supporting research. Your SME is an important collaborator and elevating what they find most valuable is beneficial to aligning your perspectives.

- **Well-cited, long-standing research:** Critically important research tends to be referenced a lot by others in the field over a long time. Some online databases include citation count as a stat on papers – this is the number of other papers that cite that paper. Be aware, however, that a paper might be cited even if the citing paper disagrees with the conclusions of the original paper. Survey these citing papers, particularly the more recent ones, to see if they support the original paper or diverge from its conclusions.

- **Recent research:** Research fields change over time as new research is done. Consider more recent research as a way of keeping you connected to recent advancements.

- **Actionable application:** In narrowing your supporting research, identify what about the research you might be able to apply to your work. Don't fall into the trap of thinking the subject of the research has to look like the thing you're building – e.g., a game. Often research can be applied through other parts of your transformational framework, giving you insights into barriers, your audience, etc.

- **Pick a perspective:** Not all the research you find will agree. Don't get stuck trying to select "The Right" research. Just make sure the research you are using is reasonably vetted and reflects a perspective that you and your team are excited to leverage together.

Learning Theory

How People Learn

Behaviorism Theory

How People Act
Based On Conditions

Social Cognitive Theory

How People Learn
By Observing Others

Cognitive Theory

How People Think

Developmental Theory

How People Learn
& Behave As They Age

Constructivist Theory

How People Learn via
Personal Experience

Instructional Theory

How to Help
People Learn

Motivational Theory

Why People Choose to
Do What They Do

Schools of Theory
in Research

If you're new to academic research, it's easy to get a little lost in the lingo. The world of academic research, even just around learning and behavior, is broad and deep. It's way beyond the scope of this book to truly illuminate this complex field. However, there are clusters of theory that often seem to come up when looking at research to inform Transformational games, and it is helpful to at least be aware of them. Here are some, along with brief layman's summaries of their meaning:

- **Learning Theory:** *How people learn.* This umbrella term is often inclusive of a broad range of theoretical schools of thought, including behavioral, cognitive, social, constructivist, and developmental theories.

- **Behaviorism Theory:** *How people act based on conditions and situations.* These theories build from core ideas that behavior is driven by conditions before or after the behavior.

- **Social Cognitive Theory:** *How people learn by observing others.* These theories focus on how individuals learn by imitating others based on social context.

- **Cognitive Theory:** *How people think.* These theories build from the core idea that internal mental processes drive learning and behavior.

- **Developmental Theory:** *How people learn and behave as they age and grow.* These theories are built on the idea that people mature through distinct stages that are characterized by distinct behavioral, psychological, and physical differences.

- **Constructivist Theory:** *How people learn via personal experience.* These theories build from the core idea that people create their own understanding of the world through experience and reflection.

- **Instructional Theory:** *How to help people learn and develop.* These theories try to give guidance on how best to design material to scaffold and support learning.

- **Motivational Theory:** *Why people choose to do what they do.* These theories try to illuminate what drives an individual's actions, desires, and needs.

Keep in mind that these theoretical schools overlap and, in some cases, compete with one another, and that these terms may mean different things to different people.

Mediating
Variables

Alternate Routes

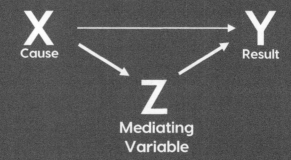

X
Cause

Y
Result

Z
Mediating
Variable

Moderating
Variables

Conditions & Knobs

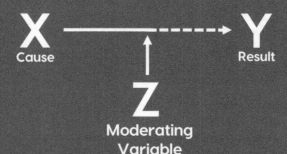

X
Cause

Y
Result

Z
Moderating
Variable

Using Research:
Mediating vs Moderating

A common struggle for Transformational games can be trying to change something that is hard to measure. Another is figuring out what will impact your transformational success, including both choices you can make in your design that might make it more effective, and also factors outside your control that might influence the outcome. Research can speak to these questions with **mediating** and **moderating** variables:

- **Mediating variables** attempt to explain why a result occurs by highlighting an intermediate factor that explains the result. *E.g., Education level (X) is predictive of salary (Y). It does not actually determine one's salary, but it does often determine your job (Z), which in turn determines salary.*

- **Moderating variables** highlight conditions which change the strength of a relationship between cause and result. Moderating variables can be qualitative attributes like gender, or quantitative, such as varying costs or rewards. *E.g., Years' experience (X) is often directly related to salary (Y) but may be moderated by gender (Z) such that women see a lower gain in salary for years' experience than men.*

You can use these research outcomes in useful ways such as:

- **Target mediating variables as player transformations.** *E.g., In designing a smoking cessation game, research points you to a mediating variable: belief in one's own ability to quit ("self-efficacy"). Targeting this belief might be a more fruitful direction than the targeting the smoking behavior directly.*

- **Use mediating variables to assess impact that is hard to observe or measure.** *E.g., You are developing a game to increase female representation in tech industries by targeting 5th graders. You'd have to wait 8-12 years to see your players' actual careers. Instead you might look to research for a mediating variable, such as self-efficacy, intent, etc. that you could test for immediately.*

- **Cater to a moderating variable through features in order to take advantage of its impact.** *E.g., You are working on a fitness game. You find research on the moderating impact of having an exercise buddy on sticking with a fitness goal. You may decide to prioritize social game features to take advantage of this relationship to strengthen your impact.*

- **Use moderating variables to narrow your focus.** *E.g., In developing a physics game, you find research that skill in basic algebra has a moderating effect on students' achievement in physics. Accounting for this may not be within your resources, so you may decide to restrict your target audience to students with a certain minimum level of algebra mastery.*

Question

#8

How will you measure your game's impact?

Assessment Plan

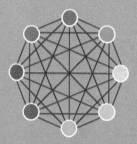

How will you measure your game's impact?

When working on a Transformational game, eventually you will face the question: "How well does it work?" Creating an **Assessment Plan** for answering this question will help your team iterate on the game during development and make claims about the game's efficacy once it's on the market.

After your game is released, many other stakeholders will also be asking this question as they decide if your game meets their needs. Some stakeholders, and your players themselves, may be interested in assessment for a slightly different reason – to understand their own growth and change facilitated by your game.

Assessment can be complex, time consuming, and expensive. To leverage assessment well, you should be thinking about your assessment plan early so that you can account for logistics and stakeholder needs, and so you can use assessment to iterate to the transformational impact you are targeting.

**Guides
Iteration**

**Powers Feedback
On Player**

**Documents
Impact**

Why
Assessment Matters

The value of assessment is multifaceted: it is valuable both during development and after release; it is valuable in regards to what it can tell us about individual players, as well as what it can tell us about the game itself.

Assessment allows you to iterate on the game's transformational design. Most game developers would not dream of releasing a game without regular playtesting of its mechanics, player engagement, and usability. Similarly, when working on a Transformational game, we should playtest for transformation. To do so requires some form of assessment.

Assessment powers feedback on the player's transformation. Your stakeholders and your players themselves will often want to see evidence of transformational progress. In order to display this progress as feedback, you will need to in some way assess players or surface information that allows your audience to infer an assessment for themselves. Understanding how to assess your player transformations will inform how you design your game's feedback systems – both what data you track and how you present that data.

Assessment documents your game's impact. Anyone making a decision to purchase or use your game based on its transformational potential will be looking for documented proof that your game works. Of course, it's quite possible that assessment shows your game doesn't work entirely as intended. That can be tough to discover but is still valuable to you and others. Future Transformational game developers may look to your game as a prior work for their own game, and assessment will inform what these future developers can learn from your efforts.

In this chapter, we'll refer to assessment for the game's sake as **evaluation of the game's efficacy** and assessment of players as **assessing player transformation**. These two angles on assessment are intimately linked – in order to evaluate the efficacy of a game, you'll often need to focus on assessing player transformation.

Levels of Evaluating Efficacy

There are a range of indicators that can be used to evaluate a game's efficacy. Some are more difficult than others to achieve. What follows are five potential levels of efficacy evaluation:

These levels of efficacy are modified from Jesse Schell's book, *The Art of Game Design* – see Appendix V.

- **LEVEL 1: Instinctual Rationalization:** *You have some internal reasoning about why the game might be effective.* A gut feeling about what should work is not without merit, as instinct can be connected to deeply synthesized experience and expertise. But it's also true that instinct can sometimes lead us astray. Going beyond instinct is the rationale behind applying a process like this Framework.

- **LEVEL 2: Theory Basis:** *The game uses research and references as a basis for its design and how it achieves player transformation.* This is essentially connecting your design to the other pieces of the Transformational Framework. It involves making design decisions that are informed by research and deep thinking on how your target transformation could be facilitated by the game's design.

- **LEVEL 3: Expert Validation:** *The game has the endorsement of experts who vouch for the game's effectiveness.* Again, if you're following the Transformational Framework, you should already have experts involved in your process who can provide this validation both during development and after release.

- **LEVEL 4: Informal Data:** *The game has been informally tested, and there is anecdotal data about its efficacy.* Achieving this level is the focus of the rest of this chapter. If you are working on a Transformational game, you should be pursuing this level throughout development and using preliminary results to inform iteration.

- **LEVEL 5: Formal Research Data:** *The game has been formally studied, and an evaluation of its efficacy has been published.* This is the holy grail for Transformational games but happens relatively rarely, as it requires both significant time and money. It's unlikely you'll be able to achieve this bar, and, even if you do, you most likely will not get results you can use to fold back into your own product for at least 2-5 years. If you do achieve this level and publish your results, you are (to me) a hero to the field, regardless of the outcomes of your study. We all learn from shared successes and failures.

LEVEL 1
Instinctual Rationalization

LEVEL 2
Theory Basis

LEVEL 3
Expert Validation

LEVEL 4
Informal Data

LEVEL 5
Formal Research Data

Levels 2 through 4 are included within the focus of the Transformational Framework.

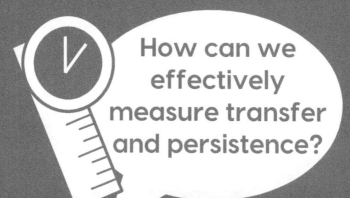

What Makes Assessment Hard

Assuming that you're aiming for Level 4 in evaluating your game's efficacy, you will need to wrestle with how to assess player transformation. Let's reflect again on our definition of a Transformational game – *a game designed with the intention of changing players in a specific way that transfers and persists beyond the game.* So when we talk about assessment, whether our focus is on the game or the player, we are really talking about variations on three core questions:

- *Does the game change players in the intended ways?*
- *How far does that change transfer beyond the game?*
- *How long does that change persist?*

In standard game development, we are accustomed to using analytics and playtests to gather data about a game's usability or engagement. Both tools are also useful for transformational games but come with these extra challenges:

It's sometimes not obvious what data you need to collect to show player transformation. If you want to know if a level in your game is too hard, you can track analytics about player performance in that level or ask for player feedback during a playtest. There is an art to analyzing this data to make good design decisions but it is often relatively straightforward to decide what data you need. In contrast, it may be less clear what data you need to collect to assess player transformation, transfer, and persistence. For example, if one of your player transformations is to improve the ability to withstand peer pressure, what data should you collect to show this transformation?

Additional resources are required to collect data that shows transfer and persistence. Often the data you will want to collect, particularly to evaluate transfer and persistence, cannot be collected inside the game or during an in-person playtest. How can you show transfer if you don't evaluate players in the real world? How can you show persistence if you don't collect data on players after the game is over? Game development teams often don't have experience with collecting data on players outside the game.

If you are not thinking about your game's assessment needs early in development, then you may find that your in-game structures do not support determining if a player transformation is happening and that you don't have the resources in place to do the out-of-game work necessary.

Progress Alone
Isn't Proof

An overly simplistic approach to player assessment is to treat questions about the player's transformational progress as a derivative of game content progression – e.g., if the player completes this level, then they understand concept X, or if the player makes this choice in the game, then they understand the value of this choice in real life. Beware this strategy.

Player progression in the game is usually not enough by itself to make claims about player transformation. Players can often brute force or stumble through game content without truly being transformed by it. Sometimes gameplay incentives can drive player behavior while in the game, but fail to change player behavior in the real world or after the game is over.

Does this mean progression in the game is useless? No. It is immensely helpful to be able to say that if the player has completed these parts of the game, then a certain level of transformation can be assumed. However, you can only support these claims *after* completing assessment that shows this correlation. To do this, use other assessment techniques to evaluate the transformational impact on players while also tracking their progression in your game. Look for a strong correlation between progression and transformation.

E.g., You are developing a game to change players' attitudes towards immigrants. You run a trial with your game that looks at pre- and post-game surveys to measure players' attitudes. You also track how much of the game players complete. You find that players that complete at least 2/3 of your game have, on average, a significant change in their attitudes. You can use this testing as positive data that supports claims about player transformation based on progression alone.

It's worth noting that not all of your players will be transformed, even when you see strong positive results overall across a group of players. Be honest about the strength of the transformation you have observed and the level of proof you have collected to confirm that transformation. No one (who is reasonable) expects your game to work to the same extent for every single player.

 In-Game
Analytics

 Observations
in Real World

 Survey
Player

 Survey
Stakeholders

 Test
Player

Example Assessment Techniques

There are many techniques you can use to collect the data needed for assessment. Here are a few to consider.

- **Track player actions in the game:** This can be a strong choice for knowledge or skill transformations that can be clearly demonstrated by the player engaging with the game mechanics. It's often the easiest method to execute because it can piggy-back off of game analytics, which is a common game development practice. However, this is a weaker option when it comes to transformations such as belief, disposition, or behavior. The validity of this assessment can be limited by the fidelity of the game to the real-world context. It is difficult to get the same feeling of stakes in a game as in real life, and it is easy for game mechanics to bias player behavior. For these reasons, players may perform differently in a game than they would in real life. Additionally, tracking in-game actions alone can't demonstrate transfer and persistence.
- **Observe player actions in the real world:** This is powerful because it can clearly show transfer and persistence. However, you often don't have a way to track what your players do outside your game. This is even more difficult in school settings where privacy concerns can shut down ongoing data collection inside or outside a game.
- **Survey player intention and disposition:** Sometimes you can't directly observe behavioral change in players. In these cases, you can ask players to report how they intend to behave or how they feel about something. These self-reported responses can sometimes be considered a predictor of future behavior.
- **Survey stakeholder impressions:** Rather than ask players directly about their transformation, you can survey key stakeholders such as teachers and parents. Since these stakeholders are also often gatekeepers for your game's adoption, understanding how they perceive your game's impact on your players can be very valuable.
- **Test the player:** Rather than simply observing players, you can prompt them to perform some task or complete a test that gives data about their transformed state. In some cases, there may be an existing, widely accepted test you can use to assess your players, such as an accreditation exam. One benefit of using 3rd party assessments is the potential to compare your players' results directly with that of non-players.

Questions to Consider

- How will you recognize player transformation?
- What techniques and metrics will you leverage?
- Do you have access to your authentic audience & context?

Formulating An Assessment Plan

The following few pages cover some tips on planning for assessment to inform development, not formal research. This is assessment that is similar to the kind of playtesting that occurs during standard game development.

Start creating your assessment plan by leveraging other pieces of your Framework to answer these questions:

- **How will you recognize your player transformations?** How will you really know if a player has been transformed in those ways? What do you need to observe and what data do you need to collect to convince yourself and others? *E.g., You're working on a game with a player transformation to change behavior around texting and driving in teenagers. Realistically, how could you observe your audience for this change in behavior?*

- **What techniques and metrics do your SME and prior works suggest you leverage?** Talk to your SME about how they would recommend assessing your target transformations. Look at the assessment practices of prior works. Since it's likely your game is going to be compared to these other interventions, it may especially benefit you to be able to compare along the same axes, leveraging similar data and methods. *E.g., Your game's transformational intent is to improve science lab skills in students. Could you leverage existing classroom instruction and evaluation methods to use as comparison and assessment for your game's impact?*

- **Do you have access to your authentic audience?** What's special about your actual target audience, and will you be able to playtest your game and assessment with them? *E.g., You're working on a game for refugee children ages 8-12 years old. You can certainly test with non-refugee kids of your target age, but your assessment data may not be relevant.*

- **Do you have access to your authentic context?** Can you access/simulate this context for your assessment efforts? If your game's intended context is very specific, it's best if you can do your assessment within this context. *E.g., You're creating a game to be used by teachers in a classroom setting. Will you be able to get teachers to test using your game in their class during development? Will those classrooms be typical of the ones where you eventually hope your game is played?*

Assessment Plan

What's inside:

- ❑ Key questions to answer
- ❑ Participant recruitment plan
- ❑ PII policies & practices
- ❑ Schedule of assessment efforts
- ❑ Data to be collected
- ❑ Data collection process
- ❑ Plan for baseline data

What's in an Assessment Plan

Your assessment plan should include the following:

- **What questions you are trying to answer about the game and the player:** Have your key questions defined so you can sanity check both the data you're collecting as well as your plan for analyzing that data to obtain the answers.

- **How your test players will be recruited:** It can be legitimately hard to find people to playtest your game. How will you find people who represent your audience? Will you compensate them in some way?

- **How you will handle personally identifying information (PII):** Depending on the age of your audience, the data you are collecting, or how your data will be used, your handling of PII may be regulated by law, so planning for how you handle your players' PII can be a big deal. Define your approach to PII and other privacy considerations based on requirements, then think about how your process will need to be set up to meet the goals of that approach.

- **Where in your schedule you will dedicate resources to assessment development:** Good assessment takes more time and effort than many people think. Establish when in your development schedule you'll be focusing on assessment. Make sure you include time to test your data pipeline.

- **What data you will track:** Justify the data you plan to use to show transformation by leveraging established norms from other prior works and input from your SMEs. Consider also tracking data on any factors you suspect may moderate your game's impact. If it would be too difficult to directly gather needed data, consider modifying your transformations or look for a mediating variable you can measure instead.

  Refer back to mediating and moderating variables on **Pg. 182**.

- **How that data will be collected:** For the data you need in order to show transformation, how will you gather this data? Think about the resources (time, money, technology, etc.) you need to execute this collection of data and also analysis of the data. Be realistic, given your resources.

- **Where baseline data will come from:** An important part of your assessment plan will be to assess players *before* they play your game so that you can show change. Do you already have baseline data available to you? If not, how will you collect it?

Assessing Half the Sky

Half the Sky Movement (HTSM) asked Games for Change to produce a suite of games on a range of concepts related to female empowerment and gender equality. HTSM is a multimedia initiative inspired by and in collaboration with Nicholas Kristof and Sheryl WuDunn, authors of the best-selling book, *Half the Sky: Turning Oppression into Opportunity for Women Worldwide*. The resulting portfolio included 3 mobile phone games, a Facebook game, and 10 mobile apps addressing topics such as education, healthcare, economic empowerment, and gender-based violence.

From the start we designed these games with a theory basis, incorporating subject-matter experts across all domains who helped determine appropriate audiences, impact goals, messaging and content. As the design evolved into game mechanics, we coordinated with evaluators to refine our assessment plans. Funding was provided by USAID, who looks to formal evaluation and assessment to demonstrate efficacy in the programs they support. Therefore a portion of our funding was allocated specifically for evaluation. The team understood that it would not be possible to evaluate the entire portfolio. Assessment can be costly and we had a fixed budget so we would have to narrow our focus to just one of our games. With one shot at demonstrating efficacy, we were very thoughtful about planning our evaluation efforts.

To determine which game to evaluate and how to prepare for that evaluation, we considered the challenges we would face: The target audiences included non-English speakers and others with low or no literacy. We would need to employ translators throughout the testing process to work around language barriers, and use images and conversation-based testing formats to mitigate literacy constraints. Audiences had limited access to technology so we needed to provide the appropriate technology on the ground while testing in remote locations. The games covered a range of topics, with content embedded in layers of levels, making it challenging for evaluators to access and understand all the content within some of the games. Some games targeted immediate transformation and others longer-term behavior change. We had to consider what measurements were possible within our year-long testing timeframe.

[1] Find references for this developer story in Appendix W.

Ultimately, we selected 9-Minutes, a game about healthy pregnancy behaviors, for assessment. The game is a simple, 9-level mobile beat-matching game designed specifically for audiences in Kenya and India. One reason this game was favored was because the topic of maternal health itself was considered to be the most far-reaching, with impact on many other social and socioeconomic forms of gender-based oppression. The topic of maternal health also came backed with lots of research and behavior theories to which we could connect our assessment. We found many of the short-term indicators of transformation around pregnancy health also were indicators for longer behavior change and saw this as a way to conduct a short-term evaluation (< 1 year) that could demonstrate longer-term implications.

Nine Minutes

9-Minutes was executive produced by Games for Change and Show of Force, developed by Mudlark Studios and published by e-Line Media.

Of all the games in the portfolio, 9-Minutes was also likely to produce the clearest indicators for assessment since it targeted only one specific topic. Our evaluators and SMEs helped us understand the research and determine what indicators for success in pregnancy health looked like. They identified 14 key messages from the game that could be tied to the trackable indicators (e.g., "drink more water") and helped us create a testing format that would address each one.

With our narrowed focus and game content mapped to indicators, we proceeded – only to discover another challenge: some participants were hesitant to engage with the mobile devices used for testing. They seemed to be nervous about breaking the phones, or struggling with how to use them. So, we had to rely even more on our evaluators to familiarize participants with the technology and help them feel comfortable during the testing process. We were grateful for the evaluators' support and, in the end, the assessment results successfully demonstrated measurable positive shifts in knowledge, attitudes, and behavioral intentions toward safe pregnancy and actions following exposure to the game[1].

This evaluation was supported by the United States Agency for International Development (USAID). The FHI 360-managed C-Change project supported the development of the 9-Minutes mobile game.

Emily Treat
Experience Strategy Director, Mad*Pow
Former VP Lab Services, Games for Change

Test
Your Plan

Just like your game itself, your assessment plan will require iteration. Before you launch your full user test to assess your game, playtest your assessment plan on a small scale and iterate based on what you observe.

1. Test a preview of your analysis.

Start with the end goal. Collecting all the data in the world is worthless if you aren't prepared to learn something from it.

Try this experiment: Generate a fake report that has charts, graphs, feedback, or conclusions you would ideally be able to create from your assessment efforts. Playtest this report. Is it digestible to others? What about the process of performing that analysis? Do you have a process in place that will realistically handle the amount of data you'll be collecting?

2. Test your data format.

As you experiment with the end-product of your data, you will also have to confront how your data is formatted. Your data format impacts whether your data is human-readable without tools, as well as how easy it is to analyze. You may find you can simplify your analysis tasks by making some small tweaks to the format of your data. Start by generating a small amount of example data in your format. Then run this fake data through your planned analysis. Is the format easy to work with? Does it allow the level of connections and cross-referencing you need to understand individual data points in the context of a larger picture?

3. Test your data collection methods.

It's not uncommon to find that your first pass at data collection is not getting you the information you want or need. You may realize that you're missing some data due to a breakdown in your process, that your survey questions are biasing your responses, or that there's an edge case you aren't tracking. Run a test where you complete the full loop of collecting data and trying to use that data to draw conclusions. Look for places to make improvements.

Good assessment takes more resources than most teams expect. Invest in these small preliminary tests and some time to iterate based on the results. This will help you get the most out of your larger assessment effort. As you playtest your assessment plan, also update your assessment schedule and allocated resources based on what you learn.

Some Questions Self-Motivated Players Ask:

❑ How can I best focus my own efforts?

    ❑ What are my strengths?

    ❑ What are my weaknesses?

    ❑ What parts of the game are particularly effective or relevant to me?

❑ What is my progress?

    ❑ What milestones have I achieved?

    ❑ How far to my next milestone?

    ❑ How does my time and effort in the game correlate to my progress?

❑ What is the real-world connection?

    ❑ What's the noticeable impact on my real-world life?

    ❑ How can I expect to measure up according to metrics outside the game?

    ❑ How do I compare to others?

Assessment as a Feature for the Player

So far, we've primarily been considering assessment as a tool for you to show your game's efficacy. Assessment can also be an important part of the game experience for the player themselves.

If your players are coming to your game because they have a personal stake in their own transformation, they may be particularly interested in assessment as a feature. You may even want to specifically think about assessment as a form of motivation for your players that may strengthen the impact of your transformation. This assessment feedback generally wants to be formative, providing ongoing feedback to the player throughout play. It also wants to complement and help sustain their internal motivation.

There is a well-known, respected body of work around motivation called **Self-Determination Theory or SDT**. SDT says that sustained intrinsic motivation requires a sense of competency, autonomy, and relatedness. Your assessment features should support these needs. Here are some questions your self-motivated players may be looking to have answered with your assessment feature:

For more on Self-Determination Theory (a theory every game designer should be familiar with) see Appendix X.

- **How can I focus my own efforts? (Autonomy)**
  Where are my strengths (things I already excel at) and where are my weaknesses (things I could choose to strengthen)? What parts of the game are particularly effective or relevant for me personally?

- **What is my progress? (Mastery)**
  What milestones have I achieved? How far do I have to go for the next milestone? How does my time and effort relate to my rate of progress?

- **What is the real-world connection? (Relatedness)**
  How does my in-game progress connect to impact on my real-world life? How does my in-game progress relate to real-world assessments by which I might be judged? How does my progress compare to others?

Coach

Judge

Stakeholder Roles

Assessment as a Feature for Others

Other stakeholders outside the player may also be interested in assessment as a feature of your game. You can divide these into two main roles – the **Coach** and the **Judge**. Note that some stakeholders (for example, teachers) may take on both of these roles.

The "Coach" Stakeholder Role

This is a stakeholder outside the player who has an interest in helping the player transform. This person wants to be able to use your assessment feature in a formative way to give relevant feedback and encouragement to the player. Here are some specific questions they may be looking to have answered:

- **Where can I help?** Where is the player getting stuck? What are their misconceptions, hang-ups, or common mistakes?

- **What can I celebrate?** What milestones has the player achieved? What transformational progress can I help the player practice, show-off, or reflect on?

The "Judge" Stakeholder Role

This is a stakeholder outside the player who needs to evaluate the player. This person wants to be able to use your assessment feature in a summative way to quickly and accurately rank, rate, pass, fail, or otherwise judge the player. Here are some specific questions they may be looking to have answered:

- **What is the overall mastery level of this player?** What can I expect from this player in the real world? How can I relate the player's mastery level to external metrics such as standards?

- **How does this player compare to others?** How does this player's skills or status compare to that of other individuals?

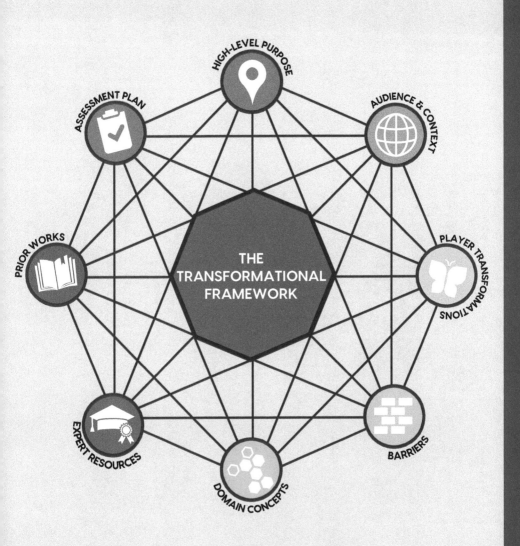

THE TRANSFORMATIONAL FRAMEWORK

HIGH-LEVEL PURPOSE

ASSESSMENT PLAN

AUDIENCE & CONTEXT

PRIOR WORKS

PLAYER TRANSFORMATIONS

EXPERT RESOURCES

DOMAIN CONCEPTS

BARRIERS

For more resources on using the Transformational Framework with your teams, visit **www.transformationalframework.com**

Where to Go Next:

- OVERVIEW -

Framework Overview Review

Now that you've reached the end of the Transformational Framework, take a moment to return to the Framework Overview chapter and review the tips there for using the Framework. In particular, keep in mind that the Framework is a non-linear tool whose pieces intersect and inform each other as you answer each of the eight questions.

- PRODUCTION -

Production Considerations

Read the next chapter for some insights into the ways that production can be impacted when working on Transformational games.

Production
Considerations

There's really no way around it: given two games of similar size and production value, a Transformational game has more moving parts, more stakeholders, and more metrics for success to hit than a similarly scoped game that is developed purely for entertainment.

For those involved in the scheduling and management of a Transformational game, it's important to recognize the potential impact of this challenge and be ready to rise to the occasion. This chapter covers a number of production considerations you should keep in mind when planning for your Transformational game development.

Extended Timeline

Additional Resources

Preparing Partners

Additional Demands For Pre-Production

It should be clear by now that Transformational games require additional effort during the pre-production period of development as compared to entertainment-only games.

Your pre-production timeline will need to be extended. Since the Transformational Framework process should be well underway – or better yet, complete – before your team digs into prototyping game concepts, this work will necessarily extend the duration of your pre-production period. It can be quite difficult to convince some teams and stakeholders that this additional time in the schedule is necessary. Take creating this space very seriously though, as it is your best defense against a major false start, which could be costlier to your schedule.

Completing the Framework may require increasing the funding and human resources you allocate to pre-production. You may need to spend funds to pay your subject-matter expert or purchase access to research papers. You will also need to dedicate human resources to drive the legwork that informs your Framework, including:

- Observing and researching your audience & context
- Soliciting and building SME relationships
- Finding and evaluating relevant prior works
- Developing a working understanding of the domain space
- Developing the format and structures for assessment

All of this work takes time and relevant expertise to do well. Consider dedicating a team member to this as your team's "Transformational Designer."

You may need to spend time preparing partners for game development. Clients and stakeholders of Transformational games can often be newcomers to games and the game development process. This creates a need for pre-production to also serve as a time for knowledge sharing from your team to partner stakeholders about what to expect during development and how to be a more effective partner.

The Game Dev Primer chapter was included to help with this process.

Additional Demands For Production

It will require more effort to keep messaging aligned. If you work on many team projects, you've probably had the experience of overhearing your manager or client describe a product in progress to someone else and thought, *"wait, that's not what we're doing"* or *"that's totally changed now"* or *"we shouldn't be promising that."* This is a classic warning sign that not everyone's visions are aligned.

Keeping everyone on the same page is even more important on Transformational games. There's the game and then there's what the game is trying to teach or change. Since there are likely to be more numerous and diverse stakeholders for your game, you will likely have non-subject-matter experts, including yourself, trying to explain or understand the transformational intent and domain content, and you'll have non-game people trying to explain or understand the gameplay of your game. You should expect to dedicate more of your attention in keeping everyone up to date and on message to avoid making claims that aren't true or setting incorrect expectations. The good news is that, if you invest time in the Transformational Framework, you will have a solid tool for the whole team for this purpose.

You will have more stakeholders involved in the content generation and review process. With more voices in your review process, it will simply take longer to parse and incorporate all feedback. You may also have more feedback from individuals inexperienced with games. Stakeholders who are less familiar with games or game development may give more challenging feedback. These different perspectives can be very valuable, but it can also slow generation and approval of game content.

Keep in mind that your experts will probably not be able to generate game content directly as this is not their area of expertise. If your SMEs are generating any of your content, expect to need to apply some developer resources to incorporate this content into the game, both in terms of adapting it for a game experience and in terms of technical integration.

Your content will need to be playtested and iterated for more than engagement. Not only does your content need to support your game experience, it also has to successfully contribute to the player's transformation. This means you might need to continue to iterate on content that playtests well for player engagement but doesn't seem to be achieving the transformational impact. You'll need to apply playtesting resources to determine if this is true.

You will have additional standards for your content and mistakes will be more critical. The stakes are much higher for the content representing your domain in the game. Entertaining dialogue is nice, unless it trades too heavily on style and confuses the key takeaways for the player. A typo is just a typo until it teaches your players the wrong spelling of a vocabulary word. A design decision made for the benefit of the game's engagement may seem like the best decision, until you find that it alienates key stakeholders because it is not authentic to the domain content of your game.

Educators' use of your game is largely dependent on the support you provide. If you want your game to be used in a classroom setting and you don't provide quality, active support for your game (including creating accompanying materials) you may struggle to gain adoption with educator stakeholders. There are exceptions, of course, as evidenced by entertainment games that have been adapted by teachers for transformational purposes beyond their intent. However this relies on dedicated teachers doing the heavy lifting of developing and promoting a model for classroom integration. In general, if you want your game to be in the classroom, budget time and resources for creating curricular content in addition to the game.

Releasing updates that address content errors is more important. Because there are often stricter qualitative and factual standards for Transformational games, there may be higher pressure to fix even "minor" content bugs that crop up after release.

This is a lot, but with the right plan, you can do it!

Entertainment Only	Transformational
Core Game Development	Core Game Development
	Content Overhead
	Expert Consultation
Pre-production	Pre-production

Pretend you have two equal buckets of resources – one is to make a traditional entertainment game and the other is to make a Transformational game. A Transformational game requires applying resources in additional ways – necessarily eating away at the resources for the core game.

Entertainment Only	Transformational
Marketing Budget	
Total Game Budget	Total Game Budget

The reality is that often the amount of money is much less for Transformational projects, and that commercial games often also have a substantial marketing budget.

Doing More...
With Less

A complaint you often hear levied against Transformational games is that the production value isn't there. These games seem to struggle to reach the level of quality that we often see in entertainment games.

You will hear lots of theories about why this is. Sometimes you will hear individuals claim that many people who work on educational games don't have good enough game production skills. Sometimes people will theorize that the academics who work on these games don't understand how important the "fun" is to a game. You might also hear that these games are constricted by the environment in which they are designed to be used and sold – that if you design for the classroom, you are limited in what you can do, or worse, that these games intentionally aim for a lower standard because they just have to be more interesting than a lesson plan or a test.

So, now it's your turn to lead a Transformational game project. And you think to yourself, that's not going to be us. We're going to make a juicy game. It's not going to have that educational feel. It's going to have a really rich feature set, it's going to have fully animated characters with completely voiced dialogue. It's going to be "fun first" – all the things that other people who don't know any better don't bother to do on these kinds of games, right?

You will soon encounter one of the most common real reasons that Transformational games often suffer in production value: They are underfunded.

Developers working on Transformational games will typically find themselves tackling a bigger problem, with more facets, and more stakeholders, but with less money. In this scenario, something will necessarily have to give. You will have to make decisions on where to apply resources. Some of the resources that would have been solely applied to developing for engagement *should* be applied to tackling your transformational design problem. This is why it's so important to have good, open, up-front conversations about priorities with your partners and team.

**Resource Costs
For Application**

**Sharing
Funds**

**Waiting
Periods**

**Reporting
Requirements**

**Research
Requirements**

The Impact of Grant Funding

If you will be working with grant-based funding for your game, be aware that this can impact your development in a number of ways:

Applying for grants requires significant resources. Writing a competitive grant requires a great deal of work that ideally involves a dedicated grant writer and the project's lead designer. You'll want to start at least a month prior to the due date – significantly longer if you need to court partners for your grant. If this is your first time writing a grant, strongly consider working with a grant writer or partnering with someone who has been through the process before.

You may be required to split the grant money. Grants often require partnerships with researchers and subject-matter experts. In some cases the parent institution of these partners will also require a cut of the grant funding in exchange for their support and credibility.

Be prepared to wait. Projects funded by grants will likely experience periods of budget and schedule uncertainty as you wait months to hear back from potential funders.

Be sure you understand and plan for the grant's reporting requirements. For many grants, regular progress reports must be written and submitted during development in order to continue to receive funding. These typically involve a narrative about the project progress thus far and plans for the next segment of work. This requires additional overhead during the project. Often grants have a final report requirement that is much more comprehensive than progress reports written along the way. It is helpful to have someone on the team monitoring what was promised in the grant to ensure that the project is fulfilling those promises.

Some grants come with formal research requirements. A formal research study has many requirements beyond the game industry's playtesting standard. This may include restrictions on how you handle data, and guidelines for testing with human test subjects, including submitting your research plan for approval to an Institutional Review Board (IRB) and restrictions on who can interact with test subjects or their data. It will likely take additional overhead to meet these requirements and will likely also require setting aside funds to specifically support this research.

Tips for Production On Small Projects

In an ideal world, you'd get more resources to work on a Transformational game, but in the real world, you often get less. In fact, often clients interested in Transformational games have very limited budgets, resulting in necessarily small projects. How can you set yourself up for success? Here are a few tips:

- 1 -
Don't Skip the Framework Process... NO REALLY.
On a small project, there is even more pressure to immediately start building. However, committing even a day or two up front to work through the Framework process can save time and frustration later. One way or another, the questions represented by the Transformational Framework will need to be answered. Skipping the process just means you will stumble through those answers as development unfolds. This increases the chance of false starts and major realignments that come from not establishing a strong shared vision of the design problem before starting to build your game experience.

- 2 -
Take the time to walk any stakeholders with responsibilities in the design process through the Transformational Framework.
No one likes to feel like everyone else is following a plan while they are out of the loop. Make sure you talk to design stakeholders early about the Framework's process and vocabulary.

- 3 -
Kickoff the project with an extended, in-person work session with the development team, subject-matter experts, and other stakeholders.
On short projects, you can't afford to slowly build up a working relationship. You really have to jumpstart it with early, intense face time. Get in the same room for 1-2 days of discussions. Make this the time when you collectively agree on the pieces of your Framework.

- 4 -
Have a plan for getting timely feedback and stick to it.
A slow feedback turnaround time can especially impact a very short project. Also, make sure you have the appropriate people to vet domain content at the appropriate milestones.

- 5 -

Narrow your transformational scope. Pick as few barriers to tackle as possible and choose very targeted player transformations. Keep the boundaries of your domain concepts as small and well-defined as possible, and limit the number of key concepts. The more you narrow your scope, the more you can absolutely focus on nailing your player transformation.

- 6 -

Make it a priority to establish a single, clear, domain authority source. This could be a person or a book or something else, but having a clear, dominant domain authority agreed upon early will streamline your process for content related to the domain material.

- 7 -

Consider design strategies that can serve you particularly well on small projects:

- **Prioritize transformation-to-genre match:** Look for a strong natural alignment of your mechanics to your domain concepts or you will end up spending additional resources trying to shoehorn together the gameplay and transformation.

- **Innovate on zero to one things:** With a short timeline, you need to pick your battles. Consider working with well-established game genres and mechanics as long as they can support your transformational goals.

- **Design for sharing:** Small projects almost always lack funding for marketing. If your high-level purpose involves creating a societal change and your marketing budget is small, spend design time on ways your game could motivate players to share the game with others.

- **Make choices that require less tailored content:** If your design requires a lot of hand-crafted content to be a satisfying experience, you may be setting your team up for crunch or failure at the end of the project. Content on Transformational projects is more costly. Set a design direction that needs less hand-authored content to reduce the burden on your team and increase the odds that you'll finish well. Less content really can be more – but your design must embrace this constraint.

Appendix
Endnotes & References

- A -

References on the Transformative Power of Games

- Whitton, Nicola. *Digital Games and Learning: Research and Theory.* Routledge, 2014.
- McGonigal, Jane. *Reality Is Broken: Why Games Make Us Better and How They Can Change the World.* Penguin Books, 2011.
- Toppo, Greg. *The Game Believes in You: How Digital Play Can Make Our Kids Smarter.*
  St. Martin's Press, 2015.
- Gee, James Paul. *What Video Games Have to Teach Us About Learning and Literacy.* St. Martin's Griffin, 2007.

- B -

Official Links for Example Transformational Games

- *At Risk.* Kognito, kognito.com/products/at-risk-for-college-students
- *Bury Me, My Love.* ARTE, burymemylove.arte.tv
- *DragonBox Algebra 12+.* DragonBox, https://dragonbox.com/products/algebra-12
- *Duolingo.* Duolingo, www.duolingo.com
- *Happy Atoms.* Schell Games, happyatoms.com
- *Harness Heroes.* Simcoach Games, www.simcoachgames.com/harness-hero
- *Never Alone (Kisima Inŋitchuŋa).* E-Line Media, neveralonegame.com/
- *Phone Story.* Molleindustria, www.phonestory.org
- *PlayForward.* play2PREVENT, www.play2prevent.org/our-games/playforward-series
- *Re-Mission.* Hopelab, www.hopelab.org/projects/re-mission
- *SuperBetter.* SuperBetter, www.superbetter.com
- *The End.* Preloaded, preloaded.com/work/channel-4-education-end
- *Win the White House.* iCivics, www.icivics.org/games/win-white-house
- *Zombies, Run!* Six to Start, zombiesrungame.com

- C -

References on Adapting Games for Transformation

- Farber, Matthew. *Game-Based Learning in Action: How an Expert Affinity Group Teaches with Games.* Peter Lang Publishing, Inc., 2018.
- Darvasi, Paul. "Ludic Learning." Ludic Learning, www.ludiclearning.org
- Isaacs, Steve. "Games and Learning." Games and Learning, gamesandlearning1.blogspot.com

- D -

More on Example Adapted Games

Assassin's Creed

- *Assassin's Creed.* Ubisoft Entertainment, assassinscreed.ubisoft.com.
- Reparaz, Mikel. "Assassin's Creed Origins – Discovery Tour Available Now as Free Download." *Ubisoft*, Feb. 20 2018, news.ubisoft.com/article/assassins-creed-origins-discovery-tour-available-now-as-free-download.
- Green, Nate. "Teaching the American Revolution with Assassins Creed III." *Social Media in Education*, Feb. 27 2013, socmeded.blogspot.com/2013/10/yes-i-played-assassins-creed-iii-in.html.
- de Rochefort, Simone. "Assassin's Creed Origins' Discovery Tour lets the beauty of Egypt shine." *Polygon*, Feb. 14 2018, www.polygon.com/2018/2/14/17008318/assassins-creed-origins-discovery-tour-impressions.

Gone Home

- *Gone Home.* The Fullbright Company, gonehome.game.
- Farber, Matthew. "Gone Home: A Video Game as a Tool for Teaching Critical Thinking Skills." *KQED*, Jan. 16 2015, www.kqed.org/mindshift/38968/gone-home-a-video-game-as-a-tool-for-teaching-critical-thinking.
- Darvasi, Paul. "Gone Home Lesson 1: Writes of Passage, Annotating a Foyer and Screenshot Citations." *Ludic Learning*, March 29 2014, www.ludiclearning.org/2014/03/29/annotating-the-foyer-towards-a-close-playing-of-gone-home.

Minecraft

- *Minecraft.* Mojang, minecraft.net.
- *Minecraft Education Edition.* Mojang, education.minecraft.net.
- Murray, Jacqui. "Minecraft in the Classroom Teaches Reading and More." *TeachHUB*, www.teachhub.com/minecraft-classroom-teaches-reading-writing-problem-solving.
- Gallagher, Colin, editor. *An Educator's Guide to Using Minecraft in the Classroom: Ideas, inspiration, and student projects for teachers.* Peachpit Press, 2014.

- E -

A Real-World Example of Game Iteration

- Vollmer, Asher. Wohlwend, Greg. "The Rip-offs & Making Our Original Game." *Threes*, asherv.com/threes/threemails/.
  The mobile puzzle game *Threes* (2014) was a big hit when released. With that success came many copy-cats who were able to very quickly clone the complete *Threes* game. In responding to these copy-cats, the creators published a blog post detailing the extensive iteration they went through to arrive at their final design. It is a great window into the art and subtlety of iteration.

More on Playtesting

- Playtesting Workshops. *Playtesting Workshops*, playtestingworkshops.com.

- Chamberlin, Barbara. "Trying Very Hard to Make Games That Don't Stink: User Testing at the NMSU Learning Games Lab." NewMexicoStateU Channel, YouTube, 11 Nov. 2010, www.youtube.com/watch?v=qx6lpeaUPSc.

- Patton, Shawn. "The Definitive Guide to Playtest Questions." *Schell Games Blog*, Schell Games, April 27 2017, http://www.schellgames.com/blog/insights/the-definitive-guide-to-playtest-questions.

Example Play Style Taxonomies

Bartle Taxonomy of Player Types
A classification of players based on their preferred actions in a game: Killers, Achievers, Explorers, and Socializers.

- Kumar, Janaki, et al. "Bartle's Player Types for Gamification." *The Interaction Design Foundation*, July 2018, www.interaction-design.org/literature/article/bartle-s-player-types-for-gamification.

- Bartle, Richard. "Hearts, Clubs, Diamonds, Spades: Players Who suit MUDs." 1996.

VandenBerghe's 5 Domains of Play
Based on psychology's "Big Five" model of personality traits: **O**penness to new experiences, **C**onscientiousness, **E**xtraversion, **A**greeableness, and **N**euroticism (OCEAN).

- VandenBerghe, Jason. "The Five Domains of Play." *Dark Lorde*, 2012. www.darklorde.com/the-five-domains-of-play.

- VandenBerghe, Jason. "The 5 Domains of Play: Applying Psychology's Big 5 Motivation Domains to Games." GDC, 2012. www.gdcvault.com/play/1015595/The-5-Domains-of-Play.

Quantic Foundry's Gamer Motivation Profile
A gamer motivation model driven by data collected from players that posits six main motivation groups: Action, Social, Immersion, Creativity, Mastery, and Achievement.

- Yee, Nick. "Our Gaming Motivation Data Distilled into a 20-Minute Talk." *Quantic Foundry*, 2016. quanticfoundry.com/2016/04/07/gdc-talk.

References for "Designing for Rural Ethiopia"

- Hammer, Jessica. "*Jessica Hammer*." Jessica Hammer, replayable.net.

- Hammer, Jessica. "G4C13: Stronger Together: Helping Ethiopian Girls Help Themselves" *Games for Change*, You Tube, July 2 2013, www.youtube.com/watch?v=9fWeNLbFk9E.

- Johnson, Jason. "In Ethiopia, One Game Design Professor Believes that Young Girls Hold the Key." *Kill Screen*, July 3, 2013, killscreen.com/articles/ethiopia-one-game-design-professor-believes-young-girls-hold-key.

References on Human-Centered Design

- IDEO.org. *The Field Guide to Human-Centered Design.* IDEO.org / Design Kit, 2015.
- LUMA Institute. *Innovating for People Handbook of Human-Centered Design Methods.* LUMA Institute, 2012.

References on Bloom's Taxonomy

- Bloom Benjamin. et al. Taxonomy of Educational Objectives: The Classification of Educational Goals. Handbook I: Cognitive Domain. 1956.
- Krathwohl, David R. A Revision of Bloom's Taxonomy: An Overview. *Theory Into Practice* 41(4), 2002, pp. 212-218.
- Bloom's taxonomy. *Wikipedia,* wikipedia.org/wiki/Bloom's_taxonomy.

References for "Transformations with Happy Atoms"

- *Happy Atoms.* Schell Games, happyatoms.com.

References for "The Barriers of Lexica"

- *The World of Lexica.* Schell Games, schellgames.com/games/the-world-of-lexica.

- M -

More on How Games Embody Concepts

- Gee, James Paul. *What Video Games Have to Teach Us About Learning and Literacy.* St. Martin's Griffin, 2007.
- Bogost, Ian. *Persuasive Games.* The MIT Press, 2007.

More on Educational Standards

Academic standards are benchmarks that define what students should know and be able to do at specified grade levels. It is not uncommon for Transformational game stakeholders to desire to hit these standards, because application to standards is one way teachers and school districts make decisions about what tools to use in their classrooms. Here are some example standards well-known in the U.S. in 2018:

- Common Core Standards. *Common Core State Standards Initiative,* www.corestandards.org.
  Typically in the U.S. when people talk generally about "standards" they are referring to the Common Core State Standards Initiative. The Common Core provides a proposed unified outline of what students should learn in the domains of Mathematics and English Language Arts (ELA). The Common Core standards were largely adopted by states in the U.S. but are considered controversial politically and socially in some circles.

- Next Generation Science Standards: For States, By States. *NGSS Lead States,* www.nextgenscience.org.

- CSTA K-12 Computer Science Standards. *Computer Science Teachers Association,* www.csteachers.org/page/standards.

More on Concept Maps

- Novak, Joseph D. Cañas, Alberto. J. "The Theory Underlying Concept Maps and How to Construct and Use Them.", *Technical Report IHMC CmapTools 2006-01 Rev 01-2008, Florida Institute for Human and Machine Cognition,* 2008.

References for "The Domain of Water Bears"

1. *Water Bears.* Schell Games, waterbearsgame.com.
2. Tekinbaş, Katie Salen. Gresalfi, Melissa. Peppler, Kylie. Santo, Rafi. *Gaming the System: Designing with Gamestar Mechanic,* The MIT Press, 2014. mitpress.mit.edu/books/gaming-system

References for "Night Shift's SME"

1. *Night Shift.* Schell Games, schellgames.com/games/night-shift.
2. Mohan Deepika, Farris Coreen, Fischhoff Baruch, Rosengart Matthew R, Angus Derek C, Yealy Donald M et al. Efficacy of educational video game versus traditional educational apps at improving physician decision making in trauma triage: randomized controlled trial. BMJ 2017; 359 (doi: BMJ 2017;359:j5416)

- R -

Example Reviews of Related Interventions

- What Works Clearinghouse (WWC): ies.ed.gov/ncee/wwc
  This site maintained by IES at the US Dept of Education reviews the existing research on different programs, products, practices, and policies in education.

- S -

More on Reading Research Papers

- Raff, Jennifer. "How to read and understand a scientific article." *Violent Metaphors*, 2014. violentmetaphors.files.wordpress.com/2018/01/how-to-read-and-understand-a-scientific-article.pdf.

- "RAND's Standards for High-Quality Research and Analysis." *RAND*. www.rand.org/about/standards/standards_high.html.

- T -

References for "Lessons Learned in Research"

1. Redd, Nola Taylor. Fake science paper about "Star Trek" and warp 10 was accepted by 'predatory journals.' *Space.com*, Feb. 13 2018. space.com/39672-fake-star-trek-science-paper-published.html.

2. Morrill, Brooke A., Madden, Gregory J., Wengreen, Heidi J., Fargo, Jamison D., Aquilar, Sheryl S. "A randomized-controlled trial of the Food Dudes program: Tangible rewards are more effective than social rewards for increasing short- and long-term fruit and vegetable consumption." *Journal of the Academy of Nutrition and Dietetics*, vol. 116, no. 4, 2016, pp. 618–629., doi:10.1016/j.jand.2015.07.001.

   Morrill, Brooke A., Madden, Gregory J., Wengreen, Heidi J. "The FIT game: A low-cost approach to increasing fruit and vegetable consumption in school." *Preventive Medicine*, , vol. 68, 2014, pp. 76–79., doi:10.1016/j.ypmed.2014.04.015.

   Morrill, Brooke A., Madden, Gregory J., Wengreen, Heidi J., Aquilar, Sheryl S., Desjardins, E. Anne. "Gamification of Dietary Decision-Making in an Elementary-School Cafeteria." *PLoS ONE*, vol. 9, no. 4, Sept. 2014, doi:10.1371/journal.pone.0093872.

3. Wansink, Brian, & van Ittersum, Koert. "The visual illusions of food: Why plates, bowls, and spoons can bias consumption volume. " *The FASEB Journal*, 20, A618, 2016. doi:10.1096/fasebj.20.4.A618-c.

4. Painter, James E, et al. "How Visibility and Convenience Influence Candy Consumption." *Appetite*, vol. 38, no. 3, 2002, pp. 237–238., doi:10.1006/appe.2002.0485.

5. Newburger, Emma, and Nicholas Bogel-Burroughs. "New Controversies Emerge Surrounding Cornell Professor's Fundraiser and Studies." The Cornell Daily Sun, 5 Mar. 2018, cornellsun.com/2018/03/05/new-controversies-emerge-surrounding-cornell-professors-fundraiser-and-studies/.

Some Online Sources for Research Papers

- **PLOS ONE:** journals.plos.org/plosone
  A multidisciplinary open-access journal, PLOS ONE publishes primary research (including interdisciplinary and replication studies as well as negative results) based on high ethical standards as well the rigor of the methodology and conclusions reported.

- **Google Scholar:** scholar.google.com
  A central search for scholarly literature that includes many disciplines and sources (articles, theses, books, abstracts and court opinions) from academic publishers, professional societies, online repositories, universities, and other web sites.

- **Research Gate:** researchgate.net
  A social network for scientists and researchers to share papers, ask and answer questions, and find collaborators.

Basis for Levels of Efficacy

Schell, Jesse. *The Art of Game Design: A Book of Lenses*, Second Edition. A K Peters Ltd, 2018., p. 509.

References for "Assessing Half the Sky"

1. Games For Change. "'9 Minutes' Mobile Game Evaluation Demonstrates Positive Change for Pregnant Women." *Games For Change*, 1 Mar. 2013, gamesforchange.org/blog/2013/03/01/9-minutes-mobile-game-evaluation-demonstrates-positive-change-for-pregnant-women.

More on Self-Determination Theory

Self-Determination Theory (SDT) is one of the most important theories of human behavior of which designers working on games, and particularly Transformational games, should be aware. There are many, many resources out there on SDT, but here are a select two that are foundational for work in Transformational game design:

- Deci, Edward L., and Richard M. Ryan. "Self-Determination Theory: A Macrotheory of Human Motivation, Development, and Health." *Canadian Psychology/Psychologie Canadienne*, vol. 49, no. 3, 2008, pp. 182–185., doi:10.1037/a0012801.

- Niemiec, Christopher P., and Richard M. Ryan. "Autonomy, Competence, and Relatedness in the Classroom." *School Field*, vol. 7, no. 2, 2009, pp. 133–144., doi:10.1177/1477878509104318.

About
Carnegie Mellon University
ETC Press

The **ETC Press** was founded in 2005 under the direction of Dr. Drew Davidson, the Director of Carnegie Mellon University's Entertainment Technology Center (ETC), as an academic, digital-first (but not digital only), open-access publishing imprint.

What does all that mean? The ETC Press publishes academic and trade books and singles, textbooks, academic journals, and conference proceedings that focus on issues revolving around entertainment technologies as they are applied across a variety of fields. Our authors come from a range of fields: some are traditional academics, some are practitioners, and some work in between. What ties them all together is their ability to write about the impact of emerging technologies and its significance in society.

In keeping with that mission, the ETC Press uses emerging technologies to design all of our books, and Lulu, an on-demand publisher, to distribute our e-books and print books through all the major retail chains, such as Amazon, Barnes & Noble, Kobo, and Apple. We also work with The Game Crafter to produce on-demand tabletop games. We don't carry a physical inventory. Instead, each printed copy is created upon purchase.

The ETC Press is also an open-access publisher, which means every book, journal, and proceeding is available as a free download. We're most interested in the sharing and spreading of ideas. We also have an agreement with the Association for Computing Machinery (ACM) to list ETC Press publications in the ACM Digital Library.

Because we're an open-access publisher, authors retain ownership of their intellectual property. We do that by releasing all of our books, journals, and proceedings under one of two Creative Commons licenses:

- **Attribution-NoDerivativeWorks-NonCommercial:** This license allows for published works to remain intact, but versions can be created.
- **Attribution-NonCommercial-ShareAlike:** This license allows for authors to retain editorial control of their creations while also encouraging readers to collaboratively rewrite content.

This is definitely an experiment in the notion of publishing, and we invite people to participate. We are exploring what it means to "publish" across multiple media and multiple versions. We believe this is the future of publication: bridging virtual and physical media with fluid versions of publications as well as enabling the creative blurring of what constitutes reading and writing.

About
The Author

Sabrina Haskell Culyba is an independent designer with experience on a wide range of products including games, theme park rides, animatronics, and toys.

Sabrina worked at Schell Games for over a decade, where she honed her interest and expertise in Transformational games. In her role as a Principal Designer at Schell, she provided creative direction and management for projects as well as helped the studio establish and refine design best practices, particularly for transformational experiences such as educational games.

Her game credits include Disney's *Pixie Hollow Online* MMO (2009), Interbots' *Let's Make Shapes!* (2010), SeaWorld's *Race for the Beach* experience (2011), Interbots' *Touch & Say* (2011), Play2PREVENT's *PlayForward* (2012), Amplify's *The World of Lexica* (2014) and *Planet Planners* (2014), the Pittsburgh Zoo & PPG Aquarium companion app (2017), and Schell Games' *HoloLAB Champions* (2018).

Sabrina has been a speaker and workshop leader at a number of conferences, including the *Games for Change Festival*, *Serious Play*, and *Meaningful Play*. She has a penchant for getting involved in game jams, including organizing Transformational game jams as well as a long-standing involvement with Global Game Jam, where she currently coordinates Regional Organizers all over the world.

Sabrina lives in Pittsburgh, Pennsylvania – a lovely city which you should definitely visit. She'd be especially glad to hear from you if you'd like to talk about collaborating on a Transformational project, running a Transformational game jam, or sharing the Transformational Framework through a workshop with your team.

She sincerely hopes this book will help you create something that you're proud of that will help change the world.

Let her know if it did: heyosabrina@gmail.com